Voices of CONSEQUENCES
ENRICHMENT SERIES

Unlocking the Prison Doors

(12 Points to Inner Healing and Restoration)

By: Jamila T. Davis

Volume 1

VOICES
INTERNATIONAL PUBLICATIONS

Voices of Consequences Enrichment Series
Unlocking the Prison Doors: 12 Points to Healing and Restoration

Copyright © 2012 by Jamila T. Davis

This book is a nondenominational, faith-based, instruction manual. It was created to inspire, uplift and encourage incarcerated women to overcome the dilemmas that led to their imprisonment and to provide instructions to help them obtain emotional healing. The author shares the strategies she has utilized, both spiritual and non-spiritual, to gain emotional wholeness. This book is not written to promote any set of religious beliefs, although it does encourage readers to be open to receiving assistance from their "Higher Power" as they know Him.

The author of this book does not claim to have originated any techniques or principles shared in this book. She has simply formulated a system of proven strategies, from her research and experience during imprisonment, that her readers can utilize to obtain healing and restoration. A comprehensive list of references used to create this work is located in the back of this book. Readers are encouraged to use this reference list to obtain additional books to further their learning experience.

Printed in the United States of America
First Printing, 2012

Library of Congress Control Number: 2012941665
ISBN: 978-09855807-0-4

Voices International Publications
196-03 Linden Blvd.
St. Albans, NY 11412
"Changing Lives A Page At A Time."
www.vocseries.com

Typesetting and Design by: Jana Rade www.impactstudiosonline.com
Edited by: Ann Lockwood, Kat Masurak and Theresa Squillacote

DEDICATION

This book is dedicated to the many incarcerated women who, like me, have had enough, along with those who desire a better life and sincerely want to change!

This book is also dedicated to men and women involved in law enforcement, criminal prosecutions, and those who render judicial decisions throughout our country. You have the authority and power to make a significant difference in our lives. We need you! Yes, even when we fall short, your concern and your helping hand have the ability to lift us up and lead us onto the right path in life. You are important to our future! We do care about what you say and think about us. Please, lend your hand and provide us with the resources and encouragement we need to become better individuals. Together we can make a difference that affects our entire country. Together we can inspire change among ourselves and so many others! Together we can become examples that will interrupt the destructive cycles that exist in our society and our prisons – breaking the chains and barriers to positive change!

Will You Give Me Another Chance?

Written By: Jamila T. Davis

Dear Sir or Ma'am,

To you I may be that numbered file that's stacked high on your desk
That represents the wrong I've done, in the midst of all my mess.
Yes, I've done my share of things that don't make me very proud,
Trying to be a "people-pleaser," moving with the wrong crowd!
And I know you probably view me as a villain or a crook;
But I ask you not to judge me by the cover of the book.
I do have a name and an identity. I have a story to tell!
There's a reason behind the story why I landed up in jail.
And no, I'm not getting ready to give you a lame excuse.
But I got to tell you, I've been through a lot! I've suffered so
much abuse!
All I ever wanted was to be accepted; to be loved.
Instead, this life done beat me down. I've been pushed, and I've
been shoved!
This story I tell, it started from the very day of my birth.
Life for me ain't been no crystal stair, since I came into this
Earth!
So many disappointments! So much hurt, and so much shame.
That led me down this criminal path I thought would ease my pain.
The more I tried to escape, the bigger the hole I dug.
If I could have only found that one who'd stop and show me love!
Could you imagine what it's like from youth to be told that you
would fail?
"Little girl, you'll never be nothing, you gonna end up right in jail!"

And I believed them when they said, "You're a liar and you're
  a cheat!"
And guess what? I became those very words that led to my defeat!
Then I stood before you, listening to words I recognized.
The way that you described me, am I garbage in your eyes?
Hey, I don't want to be that person you talked about in your speech!
I've got goals and I have dreams that I need your help to reach!
Yeah, I know it's easy to lock me up, and throw away the key.
But what about you stopping and helping me become a better me?
Don't just give me a place to sit, give me the resources I need to
  change.
And please don't place them far away; make sure they're within
  my range!
Have you ever messed up? Have you ever made a mistake?
Has life been always peaches and cream or like a piece of cake?
Was there ever someone special who offered you a hand?
And if so, what effects did it have in your becoming a woman
  or a man?
All I'm really looking for is a chance to become my greater self!
I know I can do it with the right tools and a little of your help.
Do you know how very much your encouraging words would mean?
They could change my entire life and make a difference that
  can be seen!
Please don't give up on me; I promise I'll do my best!
Don't lock me up and throw me away, like they do to all the rest!
I'm sorry! I didn't mean it! I really want to change!
I was wrong! I make no excuse! I accept the blame!
Please view me as you should, as someone whose life you can
  enhance.
Please oh please, Mr. Sir or Ma'am,
Will you give me another chance?

MY ACKNOWLEDGEMENTS

*First, I'd like to give thanks to God. Without Him, nothing is possible! Thank you, Lord, for allowing me to view my greatest obstacle, my incarceration, from Your perspective. In the midst of this fiery storm, You allowed me to discover my purpose. Now I can truly see; there IS purpose in my pain. You've allowed me to see that You are perfect and that You never make mistakes. Thank You for the storm and the rainbow that resulted from it. I now dedicate this book and the entire *Voices of Consequences Enrichment Series* to You. May it be used to glorify and uplift Your Name.

*Thank you, Mom and Dad, for the gift of life. I've cost both of you so much pain and hardship. Regardless of how I greatly disappointed you, you never left me or abandoned me. You've shown me through your actions what the true definition of unconditional love is. I will now pass the gift of love you have given me down to my children. May God forever keep you, guide, and bless you, and may He restore all that the locusts have consumed. I pray that this time around I will finally be able to make you proud.

*Thank you also goes to my two wonderful children, Kywuan and Diamond. You both have had to endure so much. I am so very sorry that I missed out on some of the prime years of your life. Thank you for loving me regardless. I pray that one day we will be able to make up for lost time.

* Thank you, Judge Carter, from the Santa Ana, California District Court. There are not many judges in this world who are quite like you. I'll never forget the day I came into your courtroom,

and you delayed my hearing to get off the stand and attend to the man whom you had let out of prison who was a heroin addict. I saw that spark of love in your eyes and heard the compassion in your voice as you asked him about his progress. Then, before you sentenced me, I will never forget how you played my music video for the entire courtroom to hear and see. You bopped your head to the music and you complimented me on my writing skills. You told me you believed in me and you saw success in my future. That day, Your Honor, you touched me. Those few words changed my life! I want to help others like you helped me. You inspired me to produce my best. This one goes out to you. Thank You.

*Thank you, Judge Linares, from the Newark, New Jersey District court, for allowing me the opportunity to get out of jail on bail and giving me the opportunity to go back to school. Without your decision to permit me to go to Lincoln University, I would have never been able to have the skill set to complete this book. My greatest desire was to show you my gratitude and appreciation by allowing you to see my reformation. Prayerfully, this book and this series will show my passion, dedication, and commitment to becoming a better me!

*Thank you, Donna Gullucio and Jenny Kramer, US Assistant District Attorneys, from Newark, New Jersey. You have both pushed me to realize my potential. Standing in front of you and hearing you passionately speak about my faults woke me up to the realization that I truly needed to change. I no longer wanted to be that horrible person you described. I took your criticism and analyzed my faults. I worked diligently to improve my flaws, and as a result of my discoveries, this book was produced. It wouldn't be possible without you, so I thank you. My only request is that you keep your hearts open and use this book as a reminder that there are some in the world who make mistakes in life, yet still will be granted the ability to change. Lend your hand of support and your words of encouragement. What you think about us *DOES* matter! What you say can, and will, make a difference. Hopefully, I will one day make you both very proud! God Bless.

*Thank you, Dawn Breedon, for inspiring me to go to Lincoln University. You are one of the greatest mentors I could ever have. Who would have ever thought I would meet you at the Bergen County Jail? You did not discriminate against me even though I stood before you in a prison jumpsuit seeking your help. Instead, you picked me up during one of my lowest points in life. For that alone I'm truly grateful, and I aspire to be just like you! You've touched so many lives of men and women who have been through the jail system. When I read your book, *Remember to Breathe*, I cried. You convinced me that I could make it regardless of all my bruises. I will never forget you! May your light forever shine.

*Thank you, Pastor Perry Mallory, for helping to make this project possible. You took the time to love me, mentor me and teach me how to become a better person. I greatly appreciate you. May God forever keep His arms of protection around you.

*Thank you, Carmen Wilkes, for being there for me! Our late nights up on the bunk in our cell will never be forgotten. I'm tossing you the ball. Take *The Voices of Consequences Enrichment Series* to the next level. There are a lot of Carmens and Jamilas in the world who really need us!

*Thank you, Shalyce Davis, the little sister that I never had. I love you so much. I will never forget the day you came into my cell, when I was struggling with so much. As I told you my problems and I began to cry, you cried with me. As I saw the tears roll down your face, at that very moment, I knew you truly loved me. You sat and watched me complete this book from start to finish. You coached me and guided me through the process, and even applied the principles to your own life. When I saw how you changed, I knew we were on to something! Don't let imprisonment get you down. You are a warrior, rise up! You are going to make it.

*Thank you, Abby and Jeremiah, for always having my back. We've been through the storm, but we're still standing. I love you both so much! You mean everything to me.

*Thank you, Mich'quel "Taylor" Nolan, for guiding me through my prison mission. You have always been there to uplift and protect me. I will never forget you! Go home and blow up!

*Thank you, Tracy Kirkland. Your loyalty and friendship is recognized and greatly appreciated.

*A special thank you to my lifelong friend Craig Pittman. You always have my back. Your support is greatly appreciated.

*A special thank you to Fatima Hakim for typing this book. Your help has been essential.

*Thank you, Latanya Jones and Rhonda Turpin. I watched you both publish awesome books from jail. Thank you for showing me the ropes and teaching us all that life, even while in prison, can be productive!

*Thank you, Adrianna Ferns, Chrisilie Tillerson, Stephanie Davis, April Moore, Angie Hudson, Jasmine Clark, Gwen Hemphill, Michelle West, Anna Della Donna, Loretta Fields, Ivy Woolf-Turk, Leslie Tavolacci, Gayle Phillips-Smith, Tawana Logan, Darly Estinval, Jennifer Filpo, Nicole Pfund, Edwina Bigesby, Janay Peace, Schnita Greenwood, Virginia Douglas, Rochina Brown, and Angela Rogers. You showed me what sisterhood truly means. Return to the free world, and shine your light for the world to see!

*Thank you, Apostle John Testola and Ecclesia Word Ministries, for your prayers and inspiration.

*Thank you, Apostle Bowser and Pathway Word Ministries, for always being there for me.

*Thank you, Bishop Itiola and Fresh Anointing Ministries. Your words of encouragement carried me a long way.

*Thank you, Prophet Wesley Van Johnson. You told me I would make it through this!

*Thank you, Quadre Smith. I have so much love and respect for you. I've watched you take your imprisonment like a trooper. I'll never forget those long nights when you coached me and prepared me for this journey that we didn't even know I was going on. I watched the way you handled your 30-year sentence, and that inspired me to learn from your strength. Your intellect and kindness has touched my heart. You, too, will overcome your obstacles. May your book, *No Use for Friends*, sell millions of copies worldwide. May your latter days be greater than your former. God bless you and love to you always - your sister.

*A very special, warmhearted, thank you to Ann Lockwood for the initial edit of this book, and coaching me on becoming a better writer. Your passion and sincerity is greatly appreciated. Thank you for believing in me.

*A special warm thank you to Kat Marusak for the final edit of this book. Your help is greatly appreciated. Your kind words have inspired me.

*Thank you Theresa Squillacote for taking the time out to help me fine-tune this project. You have been so patient and kind. I couldn't ask for a better coach! May God bless you and your family.

*Thank you to Bob Brenner for believing in this project and funding the first printing of this book series. Your generosity is admired and greatly appreciate. May your gift touch many lives, and may God bless you abundantly.

*Thank you to the many women I was incarcerated with throughout my journey. You've inspired me to create this series. Please help me to fulfill my dream of women's empowerment. Let's continue to love and support each other. We're going to make it!

TABLE OF CONTENTS

INTRODUCTION
Unlocking the Prison Doors

One of the most challenging experiences that I have ever had to endure in my life was my time being in prison. Each day I awoke in confinement feeling as though I was living a terrible nightmare. In my mind, I labeled my experience as a crisis. Consequently, my new experience did become a chaotic crisis. Moving about each day, I was seized by fear, hurt, pain, anxiety and frustration. Bewildered, I never had a clue what to expect next. I wandered about in a daze for many months, asking myself, "Is this real? How did I get myself into this?" I hated my situation and, slowly, I began to hate myself.

Prison life was a tremendous adjustment for me: From my three-level, million dollar luxury condo to a 5x9 cubicle shared with a Bunkie, surrounded by 69 other women; from freedom to chains; from lavish luxury to mere survival. I had to make the adjustment on my own. Once a decision maker, I was now given orders of what to do and when I could do it. Life was no longer about glamour, fabulosity and fun; now my life was about survival and keeping my head above water. I had to learn to swim – fast - to avoid drowning!

One day while I was lying on my bunk in a deep depression, I received a revelation, "Either do your best to see the good in this experience, or spend the rest of your time in misery." It was at that very moment that I began to shift my perception.

1

As I changed my thinking, I freed myself from the chains of the constant depression haunting me. What I experienced was nothing short of a miracle. Over the next several months, I began to live again. I was able to see and experience life through a new set of eyes. I began – and continue – to live in recognition of and appreciation for what matters most in life.

I was fortunate to find my way along this dark journey, but I began to realize that many others were not so fortunate. As I served my time, I observed a consistent cycle: Women came in, were housed, left and, too often, returned. I quickly understood that prison is merely **punishment,** and does not provide a "solution" to one's problem that resulted in incarceration. I recognized that prison is mere "housing" for the "problem," and is not "rehabilitation." The "problem" includes emotionally unstable women (including myself) who had been beaten down and broken by life. It includes women who possessed so much potential yet their minds were constrained by life-imposed "stinking thinking." It includes women who allowed their environment to define them - highly influenced by parents, lovers, so-called friends, and acquaintances. It includes women who desperately wanted to be loved, to be cared for, and to experience a happy life, yet who chose the wrong paths to achieve their dreams. The women who surrounded me were not just ordinary women. They were strong, possessing courage and tenacity. Many of them were intelligent women who had committed complex crimes. They possessed passion and drive, yet all this potential was misdirected and misapplied. With no apparent resources to solve the "problem," these women, labeled as "America's trash," or "the bottom of the barrel," are tossed into the cage called "prison," and are left to struggle to survive among many other lost souls. Instead of unlocking their potential, many prisoners embark on networking, becoming a part of the largest Criminal Networking

2

Enterprise (CNE) – comprised of thousands of women from all walks of life, all with different backgrounds, but all with the same common denominator - "criminal thinking." Instead of finding healing and restoration in their prison terms, many women leave prison with new connections and new strategies to commit bigger crimes. They participate in prison board meetings, where they mastermind how they can pull off their next heist without getting caught.

Our nation's leaders, judges, and judicial committees – not to mention taxpayers - would be startled to know how many networking plans arise courtesy of state and federal funding. I have watched the formation of many of these plans, but I decided that this would not be the path I would take. I vowed to live the rest of my life as a free woman, free from having to constantly watch my back. I wanted to be successful, but this time around, I vowed to do things the right way.

The prison sentence for me was a plea from Heaven to straighten out my life and to get things together for real this time. I desperately yearned to be free, and I was able to see that I had been locked in spiritual prison long before I ever experienced actual imprisonment. I sat in my cell and determined that I wanted to be spiritually and mentally delivered, emotionally healed and set free, yet I did not know how to do it. Locked behind bars, I felt helpless, but my drive would not quit.

One day, while in despair, I was handed the book *Houses of Healing* by Robin Casarjian- a self-help book written for prisoners and one of the very few such resources. This book showed me the roots of most offender behavior. Prior to reading this book, I had no clue that the problems I faced were also faced by others who were incarcerated. *Houses of Healing* sparked life into my spirit. It provided the means to release my

3

anger, frustration, shame and guilt, ultimately leading me onto the road of true self-forgiveness. Additionally, it gave me the desire to read other self-help books, furthering my journey to complete restoration.

Through long hours of reading and studying the Bible intensely, and poring over every self-help book I could get my hands on, I uncovered the principles that brought about my release from spiritual prison. I learned how to change my thinking, to release and channel the negative thoughts that were deeply embedded within me. I was able to receive strength in my spirit that I have now transformed into an enthusiasm to share my experiences with others. Through my discoveries, I was able to tailor a set of principles and techniques that would particularly apply to others in my situation. I immediately shared my learning and techniques with many other women who were incarcerated with me. Not only did these principles and techniques work miracles for me, they did the same for the women who also learned from them. As a result, we began to see positive changes in each other.

After being sent to the Federal Correctional Institution in Danbury, Connecticut, I met Latanya Jones, an inmate who is the author of a book entitled *Cannon Love*. Latanya was finishing her sentence for bank fraud, and we were housed together in the same unit. She encouraged me to publish my discoveries in order to share them with other inmates across the country. The result is *The Voices of Consequences Enrichment Series*, a volume of which you hold in your hands.

The Voices of Consequences Enrichment Series gives step-by-step instructions on how women can achieve their dreams, even after incarceration. Unlike many self-help books that are written by individuals who have never experienced the humiliation of incarceration, this series is written by an inmate for inmates. I share in your dilemmas, and I identify with your hurt and your pain. I have slept in the same cells as you, have eaten the same prison food, watched and participated in prison fights, and, at night, pulled those same prison sheets over my head to cry, so no one could see my pain. I was that tough girl who could never let my opponent see me sweat. I moved about prison with my head held high, with my mean grill, and my New York B-bop swagger; in reality, afraid to express my true face and feelings. At first I latched onto the wrong people, trying to drown out my soul's inner cry for liberation. I walked around prison doubly locked up. I was locked up physically, and I was locked up emotionally. One day I made a decision to take my mask off, and to lift off the bandages to expose my psychological wounds. I exposed my inner vulnerabilities and, as a result, I allowed myself to finally be healed. I am no different from you. Today I ask you to take off your mask. Lend me your hand and let me help guide you through your journey to discovery. I care about you greatly, and my desire is to see you free! I have uncovered a process of healing that I know will help you, as it helped me. It is the truth you uncover through this process that will set you free!

In this book, I will share my life experiences and many testimonies of others who overcame the same challenges you now face. Many of our stories are similar to yours, making the solutions that we found to our problems, for the most part, also the solutions for your problems. We choose to share our problems with you so that you can also share in the resolutions. Many of us have learned that time in prison can be a gift and an opportunity to take the time to learn, to heal, to analyze, and to re-evaluate our lives. Our prison confinement raised our consciousness of the need to become free from the inside out. Our feelings of self pity dissolved as we learned to see God's intended purpose for our pain. We surrendered our feelings of hopelessness, guilt, shame, anger, low

UNLOCKING THE PRISON DOORS

self-esteem, fear, and powerlessness as we began to learn how to manage our emotions. Our goals moved from simply getting out of jail to a new mission to make the most of our time of incarceration in order to ensure a positive future for ourselves and for our families. This experience has become the turning point of our lives. This spiritual awakening transformed our experience from crisis into opportunity. You too can have this same experience!

Through this book, I will guide you on your journey. Unlike typical self-help books, I created this book with genuine care and compassion. This is the road map I used to overcome my dilemmas. Therefore, I'm not speaking down to you. I am with you, for we are the same. I understand your need and desire for true restoration. I thank God every day for His treasures that He revealed to me. My greatest pleasure now is to share these proven strategies and techniques with you.

Let this time of imprisonment be a "time-out" for the greatest and most important transformation of your life. Open your heart and mind with a willingness to change. Be real with yourself. All crimes come with consequences, whether they manifest instantly or in the future. The results are the same. The definition of an insane person is one who does the same things over and over, expecting different results. Don't be that insane person. Your time of incarceration is your opportunity to change and change begins inside your mind. We are each a result of our thought life: Our thoughts create our habits, and our habits become our lifestyle. In order to change our lifestyle, we must begin changing our thoughts. This book will help you recognize and identify your thought patterns, allowing you to ultimately shift those patterns to achieve a more positive lifestyle.

Many of us dream of success and a good future, yet we pursue success relying on external factors such as people, places and things. True success comes from within and not from without.

This book will help you begin to evaluate your most important asset, which is your "self." When you discover who you truly are and the power that lies within, you will be able to regain your dreams. The goal is to look inside yourself and honestly evaluate your shortcomings and any other unnecessary baggage you need to unload. Once you empty the "trash," then you can renew your mind with an abundance of wisdom and knowledge that will help you reach your goals!

We all have choices. In order to change, you must choose to change. No matter how badly our loved ones and friends want change for us, change will not happen until we make the initial choice to accept it. This choice requires that we surrender our will and seek the will of our "Higher Power." We must recognize that life will not conform to our vision, until we surrender to the will of God. God's will for each and every one of us is for us to be prosperous in every aspect of our lives, but we must live life according to God's plan.

By opening the cover of this book and reading this far, you are making a great choice by accepting the possibility of a new life. Follow me through this journey, and use this time as an opportunity to grow emotionally and spiritually, while developing your knowledge and skill sets. Outside the prison walls, it would be extremely difficult to devote such an enormous amount of time to improve "self." Return to the world ahead of the game. "Fix" yourself, so you can share your growth and lessons learned with many others who so desperately want it, but do not know how, and where, to begin! Let's make up for lost time!

Take the time to go through the steps in this book patiently. Absorb what you read by studying the contents. Take out your *Voices of Consequences, "Unlocking the Prison Doors"* Workbook/Journal and take notes as you read this textbook. This book is not written to be read straight through; it is written to be studied and experienced. Do the exercises. Meditate and place the material in your heart. Practice the principles you learn on a daily basis. Eventually they will become your habits. Those new habits will help you create a new and victorious lifestyle.

Sit back, take a deep breath and enjoy the process! You have embarked on "Mission Change." I have only one request of you: When you arrive at your destination and enter the new ground called "freedom," please share the keys and the map of the path of your journey with as many others as you can. Pass this book along. In fact, you may want to do the exercises with a group, as well as by yourself. Whatever you do, don't keep this message to yourself! As you share this message with others, the law of reciprocity will return to you an abundance of blessings and opportunities.

May your journey forever be blessed and prosperous. God Bless.

-Jamila T. Davis

CHAPTER 1

Learning to Surrender

B efore we begin this journey, let's pause a moment. Now is the time to evaluate our lives and determine if we are truly ready for change. Stop, look around and examine your environment. The walls that surround us seem so defining. Observe your peers; pay close attention to their actions. Now, ask yourself: Is this the place you want to be, or is there another plan for you, in order to fulfill your destiny? Time is ticking, the clocks aren't moving backwards, and you aren't getting any younger. How much more time can you afford to give up? So, what's next for you after this? Will you leave jail and get a good job? Will you settle down and provide for your family? Or, will you go back out and try to hustle up some cash and take the risk of being caught up in the madness again? Do you return to the old neighborhood, and pick up where you left off? Or, do you hit the streets and party like a rock star, making up for lost time? You have many options, and you make the choices. The choices you make are critical; they determine your future! And the choices you make will answer the question: "Will you return to this place and have to start again, at this very same point?" You control the answer to this question. What will life be like this time around? Will you fail or will you succeed? What do you want your life to be like going forward? Do you want success, or will you accept defeat?

Before we can begin anew, we must be ready to surrender, much like the old saying illustrates - You can lead a horse to water, but you cannot make it drink. I can expose you to the power of choice, but I can't make you choose. Only you can make the choice. You determine your destiny. It's important that you clearly understand that if you remain on the same destructive path in life, you are guaranteed that the results will not be different. Life will continue to deal you the same old hand. Ultimately, there are no exceptions! The consequences for living a life of crime are costly. Initially, you may appear to be getting ahead, but a life of crime will <u>always</u> cost you more than what you have gained. In fact, you will pay double tomorrow for what you gain today. It's not worth it! Think about this honestly: How much did you truly gain? How much did you lose? Now ask yourself the question: Was it worth it?

I would like to share a poem I wrote that I believe many inmates can identify with. The poem urges us to recall our past, and to reflect on the high price we have paid for our misjudgments:

I Surrender – A Prisoner's Cry
By Jamila T. Davis

There comes a point in our lives when enough becomes enough!
When constant troubles arise, and life is way too rough.
Like a bomb that drops, all hell breaks loose, without a person
  in sight to give us a boost.
All our poor judgments backfire in our face, and those who we
  trusted become informants in our case.
Everything we try begins to quickly fail, surrounded by these
  cinder blocks, in our new home we call jail.
On our bunks we stop and think, "How in the world did we land
  here?" That's when our problems come to light, causing
  pain too great to bear.

10

Some of us started off as that sweet innocent child.
She had two ponytails, big fat cheeks and an irresistible smile.
One day she was lured by someone she thought she could trust,
Who snatched away her youth as his hands fondled her bust.
The shame never left, the reproach settled in.
Next thing she knows she's caught up in a lifestyle of sin.
Then there're those of us who started off fine, who lived in a nice
house, whose parents were kind.
Things were great, she's headed for success! Then she met her
love, that's when her life turned into a mess.
Blinded by love, she couldn't see, had no clue this kind of love
would ruin her destiny.
Then there's one who struggled from the day of her birth,
With daddy in jail and momma on crack, since she entered this
place called "Earth."
There were many nights the cupboard was bare, she had no
food to eat.
In a quest to survive she sought love, now she rocks designer
shoes on her feet.
Her love had the money rolling in, but as a drug dealer's girl,
her new problems begin.
When the troubles came many of us tried to escape, looking for
the solutions to bypass the yellow tape.
She started with weed and it put her at ease.
But one day she discovered the weed would no longer please.
Then she tried coke, then crack, then dope.
When that didn't work she lost her hope.
Whatever it was we were all sold out!
For a moment no struggles, no worries, no doubts.
Then like a whirlwind, the storms began to come:
The things we did we thought were wise, turned out to be so
dumb.

In the storm we learned so much, no longer blind to life.
We learned that love wasn't love at all when it stabbed us like
    a knife.
Where are all our friends who were around when everything
    was up?
They're out seeking a free ride; who'll be next to fill their cup?
Things aren't what they seem to be. What we thought was an
    escape, became a tragedy.
We found out in the end we only have our self.
Some of us are left beat down and robbed, HIV done stole our
    health.
Bad choices and poor decisions led us to this very place. And on
    top of all that misery, now we got this case.
There's got to be another way. Things can't stay like this! Left
    inside this lonely place, our families greatly missed.
Pushed so hard against the walls, depression has us bound.
It is not until we get to this place that true help can be found.
Are you tired of running in circles?
Are you tired of the hurt and pain?
Are you finally convinced you must surrender because life will
    never change?
What about the kids you left behind?
Is it fair to them, that they, too, must do this time?
What about the others who hurt because of our pain? Will you
    change for them or will you stay the same?
It's time to make a choice; is enough, enough?
Are you ready to release the shackles and take off the handcuffs?
Are you ready for a brand new life? Where you can be a mother,
    a friend and a wife!
Are you ready to achieve your dreams, without having to watch
    your back? When life can finally be filled with plenty and we
    no longer suffer lack!

You can have it, it's your choice! You can sign the agreement with your voice!
I surrender, I surrender, is all you have to say. That's when help will come your way.
Are you ready to follow me now, down this road called change?
I promise, if you surrender today, your life won't be the same.
Open your mouth and throw up your hands.
With your voice release the shackles and bands.
There's nothing left but for us to say, "I give up this old life, I surrender today!"

Many of us have been in denial, which has caused us to stagnate, trapped in the same place. We don't want to admit our shortcomings, so we live a lie. We are covered with masks of deception, acting as if life is fine and everything is okay. We hide behind people, places and things and we use them to justify who and what we are. If we would admit the truth, which is hidden deep down, we'd see we are empty and lonely, caught in a high-speed pursuit for fulfillment. In reality, we are on a path of self-destruction. While we search outwardly for fulfillment, we remain unaware that the solution lies within.

For example, many of us have sought men, believing – and convinced - that our fulfillment lies with one of them. "Once I find the right man, he will complete me, and my life will be good," we say. Others turn to drugs, thinking they will provide our sustenance. There are those who pursue money, saying, "Once I get enough, I'll be okay, because money is surely the solution that will take my problems away." On this high-speed pursuit we've been racing through life, only to hit these cement walls called "prison." A place none of us ever wanted to be in. We did not want to start the next chapter of our lives here.

Where did we go so terribly wrong? It all started with a choice. Usually ONE bad decision can be identified as the very thing that landed us in prison, supported by a series of cycles, wrong thoughts, and wrong habits that brought us to a lifestyle of criminal behavior. And, of course, we had the mindset, "I'll never get caught," or "I'll do this just once, get the money and I'm done." Many of us never stopped to think about the severity of the consequences. Self-absorbed, we never thought about the lives that would be affected by our actions, including the suffering of our loved ones who would be left behind with our imprisonment. We failed to calculate the cost of our projected gain. In the middle of this mess, we now can clearly see that the crime was not worth it. Left to hold our bags of despair, many of us are lonely, with very few who really care. What is left to do? It is truly time to break free by surrendering our hearts and minds, and recognizing that this is not the way our lives are intended to be. We must change!!! We can change!!!

Change is a process that requires willingness. We must surrender our old ways in order to embark upon a new lifestyle. Aren't you tired of the havoc? Are you tired of taking one step forward, only to take two steps back? Wouldn't it be nice to live in peace, surrounded by love, and immersed in happiness? Would you like the chance to finally make your loved ones proud, and to prove your greatest critics wrong? Wouldn't it be great to be whole and to finally feel complete, without the crutches of people, places and things? That's real freedom! You have a choice, and only you can make it. The decision is yours! Choose life and surrender.

Surrender, by definition, means to give up attachment to results. Typically, we do things to receive an expected result. When we learn to surrender, we release our attachment to our expectations. We transition our efforts to control the external world to focus on our internal world, which lies within us. When we learn to surrender, we open the gateway to receive peace and restoration.

WARNING To surrender is one of the most difficult choices for people to make. Man's nature is to be in control. We believe we have all the answers, and know what is best for us. The common response is, "I'm grown, and you can't tell me what to do." Everyone has their plan and agenda. But when we reach a point of crisis, we become desperate. Then, in our desperation, we face the critical moment when we realize we are helpless to change the situation. Crises and failures lead us to fall on our knees and surrender. Hardships humble us and allow us to admit our shortcomings. Unfortunately, for many of us, things have to get really bad before we surrender and begin the search for an escape from our pain.

Surrender is acceptance. Acceptance is what relieves the pain. When we accept our shortcomings, we can find a solution to alleviate that pain. It truly is simple. If we admit our problems, we can receive help. The first step in this journey is for each of us to simply admit that our lives have become unmanageable in their current state. We must admit that we need to make adjustments and that we need help in our pursuit to change. Surrender is simply our admission that we need help.

Are you ready to break the cycles of crises and failures? Are you ready to surrender and make a change? If so, join me in saying these words: *"I admit that my life has become unmanageable. I recognize that I'm at a point in my life where I need to experience change. I realize that I cannot make it by myself. I formally surrender."*

That's it! You are now on the path called *CHANGE*. By surrendering, you have opened the doors for help to come your way. The journey will be exciting. There's so much to learn! Now you can work on your biggest asset, which is "self." Get ready and expect the best to come!

CHAPTER QUESTIONS
1) What does it mean to surrender?
2) Why is it necessary to surrender in order to move forward in life?
3) Why does it take people a long time to surrender?
4) Why is it difficult to give up control?
5) How do you surrender?

WRITING ASSIGNMENT
Explain some of the activities you were involved in that you will need to surrender and why you need to surrender them.

CHAPTER 2

Accepting Help from Our "Higher Power"

In the last chapter, we learned about the importance of surrendering our power, understanding that until we admit that our lives have become unmanageable and that we are powerless in our current state, we cannot receive the help we need to change. Change cannot occur until we desire it. When we become tired of the same old routines, an awakening occurs within us that leads us to surrender our will. This act of surrender opens the door for us to receive help. The fulfillment we have been desperately searching for in people, places, and things has been within all along!

What a profound revelation to discover that the help we actually need can be found within us! Our help comes from the divine assistance of our "Higher Power" that lies within. He is the Being that sculpted, molded, and created us. To many He is known as the Almighty God. He is our "Higher Power." Your divine Source of assistance, He lives and abides within each of us.

Religion is a controversial issue that we will not discuss in this series. Most agree that the Earth, moon, sun, and stars, as well as all the creatures that inhabit them, were created by a "Higher Power." Humans have no control over life or death. Some people are shot, stabbed numerous times, or receive many

17

other blows that should have ended their lives, yet they live. Why? Someone larger than them holds the power and control over their destiny - their "Higher Power." Just as He holds the control over life and death, He also holds our future in the palm of His hand. He permits our hardships so that we can develop a relationship with Him. He wants us to realize that we control nothing by ourselves. Our "Higher Power" desires us to reach out to Him, and then He will lead and guide us in the way which we should go.

Some of us are reluctant to call on our "Higher Power," because inwardly we are angry with Him. Many of us have faced numerous strenuous battles in life. Some of us have even lost loved ones very dear to our hearts. Because of this, we have become bitter. Our attitude has become, "If God is so good then why would he let this happen to me?" Secretly, many of us have harbored this resentment in our hearts, which has ultimately blocked God from moving in our lives.

God's ways are higher than our ways, and His thoughts are higher than our thoughts. He knows the end from the beginning, and what will happen in between. He sees what we cannot see. God is perfect. He makes no mistakes! Even when loved ones pass on, we can be assured that they are in a better place. They no longer have to deal with the struggles of this world. God loved them so much that He saved them! You cannot know what they may have had to experience if they had remained alive. Guaranteed peace is better than the suffering, hurt, and pain of this world, and because you loved them, you want the best for them, and now they have the best. We are the ones who still must strive and work hard to one day receive God's best. When we open our hearts and minds to trust in God's perspective, then we can see, "God is good, all the time."

For those of us who have endured many obstacles in life,

be of good courage. There is purpose in your pain! You have endured all that you have so that you could be molded for God's plan for your life. He indeed has great plans for you! Each difficulty that you encountered trained you to become a warrior. Through these challenges you have learned critical lessons that will help you grow as a person. Obstacles teach us what is and is not important in life. They keep us from growing complacent and self-reliant. During these times, we learn to appreciate the importance of family and love. Too many in the world today chase after the "almighty dollar." We devote our entire existence to running after money, only to die and not be able to take it with us! How ludicrous! Life is not about money. Life is about love and fulfilling our purpose. Until now, our priorities were misplaced, and our perspective on life was out of order. Look at the people we trusted, catered to, and spent our time with. Many of them are gone. They said they loved us, and we believed them, only to discover their motives were not pure. Our focus should not be on people, places, or things. Our hardships teach us that our focus and trust should be in our "Higher Power."

We are not alone in this journey! Our "Higher Power" within desires to help us. Our current misfortunes are not here by chance. They have led us to this place to gain our attention. God has been speaking to us and tugging at us, but many of us were so caught up in this busy world that we were unable to hear Him, let alone listen. However, God is a Gentleman; He does not force Himself on us. He allows us to make the choice for Him to help us. Many of us received His warnings even before incarceration. Think about it. Did you ever get a gut feeling, deep down inside, that said, "Don't go there today," "Don't trust them," "Something isn't right?" Chances are you felt it, yet you dismissed the warning as your own foolish fears. But you were wrong! God was communicating with you by dropping subtle thoughts into your mind. Those thoughts were not your own! It's like when we know something's going to happen, and then it actually does. God talks to us through our hearts and minds, and He also speaks to us through dreams and visions. It's important that we begin to listen to God, to get closer to Him. It is when we become still and "quiet" that we are able to hear His message. God has been talking to us all along, but our spirits have been so busy that we couldn't hear what He's been saying. Surrounded by these lonely walls of despair, many of us have now been repositioned to listen.

God wants to help us overcome every single one of our shortcomings. He has a great plan for all of us! He wants to place us in positions of greatness, but first we must overcome our weaknesses. If not, we will destroy the very gifts God gives us. It's like a set of loving parents who desire to give their child the best. They would not give their eight-year-old child a new car because she would not have the experience or maturity to drive it. If they gave their eight-year-old child the keys to the car, she would crash it and possibly kill herself or others. Wise parents wait until the child is old enough and obtains her driving license. Even then, before getting the car, the daughter must learn how to care for as well as properly drive the car, so that she can maintain it. God wants to give us that which we will be able to maintain. We will only inherit His gifts when we mature by overcoming our shortcomings.

God will not take from us what we are unwilling to release to Him. Again, God is a Gentleman. He only works with our consent. He will not help us overcome our shortcomings without our willingness, because that would be a violation of our free will.

Through wisdom and knowledge, we open the doors for healing. As we come into consciousness about who we truly are, and are able to see clearly, we become enlightened. This enlightenment leads us to solutions to our dilemmas. Once we know <u>what</u> we need to fix, it becomes easy to fix it. Healing cannot occur until our wounds are revealed. This process of discovery can be painful. We will need help from our "Higher Power" to get through this journey. He will help illuminate our path as He brings us into an awareness of our shortcomings, and He will comfort us as we undergo this transformation.

The goal of our journey is personal growth, moving beyond dark, emotional patterns which have caused us so much unwanted pain, into healthy habits that create inner peace. As long as we remain in a state of chaos and confusion in our minds, our behavior will reflect this negative energy, and conflicted behavior cannot coexist with peace. Conflicted behavior only generates more conflict. Peace of mind must become our target in every situation we encounter. When we direct our minds towards peace, ultimately we will receive it! Peace comes when we surrender our own will and seek God. When we direct our minds toward peace, we are programmed to achieve emotional stability regardless of the circumstances. In this way our minds become naturally programmed to view our circumstances from a peaceful perspective. Peace is always God's will for our lives.

Most importantly, as you go through obstacles, remember that all things will work together for our good. That means something good will always happen to us in the end because we passed the test. Challenges are there to test us and teach us. When we master the lesson, we pass the test and are greatly rewarded. In every crisis there lies the "opportunity" to gain. Our challenge is to recognize the good, or the "opportunity," that can come from every situation.

Let's take a look at the crisis of imprisonment. Many of us believe that this is the worst thing that could have happened to us. The thought constantly plays in our minds: "Why me?" Have you taken time to consider the good that can come from

21

this situation? For many, prison can be a hospital for healing and restoration. In prison, we can clear our minds, and learn to straighten out our priorities. In fact, many of us have been saved by prison. If we had stayed in the same destructive patterns and lifestyle as we were in previously, we could have died! God loved us so much that He saved us! He wanted us to change our thinking, so ultimately we could change our lives. God does have a plan for us! He wants us to prepare for our new position of greatness, our triumph.

For some of us, our family relationships have deteriorated because of our adverse behavior. God often uses prison to bring family members closer. Imprisonment allows us to see who truly loves us and who does not, which allows us to straighten out our priorities. Some of us have been putting the wrong people at the top of our priorities. I want to share a true story with you about a dear friend, Tracy, whom I met while incarcerated at the San Bernardino jail in California.

EXAMPLE

Tracy is a tall, slim, beautiful, light-skinned African-American woman in her early 40s. She was born and raised in Los Angeles, California. Tracy was a good woman - she did the right things and excelled in life. Tracy aspired to become a lawyer. She worked hard and put herself through law school. Tracy dated many distinguished men, but her concentration was on her studies.

One day Tracy was introduced by her best friend to Sam, her friend's cousin. Sam was an attractive younger man from Philadelphia, PA. He landed on hard times during his relocation to California and ended up in a homeless shelter. She remained friends with Sam and allowed him to use her car while he searched for a job. Eventually he started sleeping on her couch.

Although initially they were strictly friends, Sam passionately pursued Tracy, and the couple married. Tracy pushed Sam to be his best, and sacrificed her own studies to help Sam pay for college to earn his engineering degree. She became a lawyer, and Sam became an engineer. They had three beautiful children, and life was good.

Tracy grew up in the church and had a fairly close relationship with God, but she slowly began to neglect God as she focused on her husband and her career. Their lives began to go downhill after the family moved into a half-million-dollar house in an exclusive community. Tracy and Sam found themselves with barely enough money to pay the bills. Tracy, passionate about her family, desperately looked for ways to sustain the family's lifestyle. After encountering several dead ends, she began stealing the profiles of dead people to obtain credit. Tracy misused her knowledge and intelligence and compromised her integrity. By doing this, she was able to make a lot of money, which enabled her to pay her numerous bills. Life seemed good, until the Feds uncovered her scheme. Tracy was arrested, she lost her law license, and she was imprisoned.

Within the first 60 days of her imprisonment, her family situation went from bad to worse. Tracy's husband became verbally abusive to her over the phone, as he blamed her for ruining his life. Tracy's house went into foreclosure, and Sam feared losing all his worldly possessions.

Within four months, Sam started cheating on Tracy with a younger woman, who moved into Tracy's house. Tracy called her children and discovered that Sam's girlfriend was wearing her clothes and sleeping in her bed. Tracy thought she would die inside! She was so hurt! After 15 years of marriage and all the sacrifices she made, everything had gone down the drain! The man she had rescued from the homeless shelter and supported gave her his behind to kiss. She never would have expected this from him.

Tracy received a 30-month prison sentence. Upon her release, she divorced her husband and gained custody of her children. Tracy rekindled her relationship with God while she was in prison, and she continues to be deeply involved in her church. In prison she also found her purpose and now has a fulfilling career that is not only satisfying emotionally but financially. Tracy is happy and her life finally has real meaning.

At first, jail may have seemed the worst punishment, but for Tracy, and many like her, it was a blessing in disguise. Imprisonment can give us the opportunity to dissolve wrong associations and improve character defects. Life has no meaning without purpose! We can use this time in prison to discover what God has planned for us. True happiness is found when we do in life that which God intended for us to do. It is easy to discover these truths while sitting alone in our cells.

Prison doesn't have to be a dreadful experience. You hold the cards! You <u>can</u> make the best of it! Use this time to work on your "self." *YOU* get it together so life will come together. We cannot accomplish this mission alone. We need the help of our "Higher Power," to lead us, strengthen us, and help us along the way.

Are you ready to accept the guidance of your "Higher Power?" Join me in this prayer: *"God, today I invite You into my life. I desire to know You better. I admit I am powerless over my current situation and circumstances. I recognize I am in a stage of my life that requires change. I realize that I can do nothing by my own strength. I need a Power greater than myself to restore me. I now turn over all my problems and burdens to You. I ask You for the strength I need to get through this journey. I surrender my will and my expected outcome, and I turn over the results to*

You. Come into my life today. Restore my heart, mind, and soul. Show me the way You intend for me to go and provide me with the necessary help and resources to get there. Amen."

Congratulations, you are now on your way to restoration! Sit back, relax and enjoy your prosperous outcome. You have now officially opened the doors to change!

CHAPTER QUESTIONS

1) What is our "Higher Power?"
2) Why do we need a "Higher Power" to get through this journey?
3) Why do people get angry at God?
4) How can we receive help from God? What does He require of us?
5) How can our time in prison become an opportunity?

WRITING ASSIGNMENT

Write a letter to your "Higher Power?" Tell Him how you feel and what you expect or want Him to do in your life. Be specific.

CHAPTER 3

Getting to the Root of the Problem - "Who Am I?"

We live in an age where so many people are not happy with who they are. They look at themselves in the mirror and their reflection displeases them. Deep inside their hearts, they are plagued with the belief, "I'm not good enough," because their perception of themselves has become defiled by the standards of society.

When we turn on the television, we are bombarded by images of people idolized by this world, creating the deceptive belief that if we look like these people, dress like them, and live their lifestyles, we will achieve success and happiness. In turn, we spend thousands of dollars and tremendous amounts of time and effort attempting to figure out a way to achieve these worldly standards. Our lives become consumed by chasing a false belief of self-worth, leaving few of us who desire to be ourselves. The majority adopt a false sense of self, assuming the identity of someone else. Sadly, this false identity becomes deeply embedded, blinding people to the truth of who they really are.

The world is populated with millions of people who move about with masks on their faces. Very few stand up and become leaders, secure in their own identity. The vast majority become "people-pleasers," becoming the person they think society wants them to be. "If I obtain this degree, I'll make daddy happy." "If I lose this much weight, I'll finally get a husband." "If I have this amount of money, I'll finally be fulfilled." "If I act like this, I know they will love me." These common misconceptions lead us on a misguided journey, searching for fulfillment that cannot be found externally. Strongly influenced by wrong values, our lives lie in disarray, and we are left with no true identity.

Prison life magnifies this lost identity syndrome. Think about it. How many stories have you heard others tell about who they were and what they were in the free world? But then you discover, when someone comes to prison who knows them from the streets, the stories were all lies. They told other people's life stories and adopted them as their own. Some of these people are so convincing that they even start to believe their own lies! They move about trapped in the identity of someone else. They hide behind this false image because they are afraid to be themselves. They believe that if they tell others who they are, people will not like them. They fear rejection. They so desperately want to be loved and accepted, so they are willing to live a lie to receive the esteem of others.

Restoration cannot occur until we remove our masks. When we unwrap the layers of false identities that encumber us, we can finally ascertain who we truly are. This task is not easy because many of us have adopted false identities over the years, creating a stronghold wrapped tightly over our true selves. Removing the numerous deceptions and discarding the excess baggage we've unconsciously accumulated over the years can be a painful process. Exposure makes us naked, which magnifies our insecurities. This experience can also be frightening, which can make us reluctant to embrace it. Many of those who start out on the journey of change pull back because they are unwilling to endure the pain. It is man's nature to avoid feeling hurt, which is one reason that so many people seek the use of drugs and alcohol. They don't want to deal with the pain in life. Instead of fixing problems, they try to suppress them, hiding them deep down inside. Then they put on another mask to cover up those problems. When we create such an ongoing cycle, we become delusional, not knowing who we truly are.

In order to heal we must be willing to expose the truths of who we are, and begin to learn how to love "self." Loving "self" brings us into acceptance of who we are and helps us to identify our strengths and good qualities. As we learn how to become content with who we are, it allows us to grow and nurture a sense of self confidence. Our goal in this series is to uncover and reveal "self," identify our bad habits and weaknesses, and discontinue them. Our goal is to also discover our strengths and good qualities, magnify them, and attract more. We must take these steps in order to achieve wholeness. When we cleanse our hearts and minds of deception, we allow ourselves the opportunity to discover the truth and the beauty of "self."

Many of us have asked ourselves, "How did my life disintegrate into such disarray?" We cannot efficiently move forward until we truthfully answer that question. To discover freedom, we must discover the root of our problems. How did all this deception begin? In this chapter, we will explore the truths of who we are. We will unravel all the self-made bandages that we used to cover our hidden wounds. We will take off our masks and identify the truth of who we are.

We were all made in the wonderful image of God. Each of us was designed with unique gifts and talents. Each of us is predestined with a purpose or an assignment. God made us as we are so we could manifest His desired results here on Earth. When we discover what this predestined assignment is we will discover our purpose. Working in this purpose brings about fulfillment of an inner void that nothing else can fill. We become joyous about life and happy in our existence. Each of us has a common enemy whose assignment is to kill, steal, and destroy, who some call Satan or the devil. His job is to distract us and keep us from achieving our purpose. This enemy has been busy working since the beginning of time. He is both clever and deceptive, causing many of us to fall into his traps and fail in our purpose. He has plotted and schemed against each of us since we were little children. He has also entrapped others to do malicious things to us, starting in our youth, causing many of us to be the way we are today. Our enemy's mission is to distort our minds and our thinking, and to cause our self-destruction. As they say in the streets, "Now it's time that we peep game." It's time to open our eyes and see those deceptions to which we have been blind. As we ascertain the truth about our beginnings, we will discover how and where we took the wrong path.

Our enemy is calculated and seasoned in his endeavor to sidetrack us. He has purposely planted misfortunes and inflictions that we endured as children. These pre-determined events were intended to destroy us and ultimately have influenced the person we have become today. It is so important to come into an awareness of our enemy and to understand the premeditated events we suffered that altered our lives. When we recall these events from our past, we can easily shift from being the victim to the victor. These events have imprinted on us a negative stigma that has defiled us. Today we must prepare to remove the defilements of our past, rise up and destroy the strongholds of deception that have gripped us, and come into consciousness of the truth as it really is!

Exposing the plot of the enemy and replacing our negative thoughts with the truth enables us to renew our minds. With our minds renewed, our thoughts are changed, and we can see the light even in the midst of our darkness. This light will lead us to discover our new life, which is our God-given destiny of prosperity. It is God's desire that we become whole, with nothing missing and nothing broken in every aspect of our lives. It is this wholeness that will satisfy us, eliminating every inner void we may have.

In order to move forward, we must first go back and examine how we became the person we are today. For many of us, it is difficult and often painful to look back at our childhood experiences because of the abuse and neglect we suffered. Some of us grew up with hardship and fought to overcome the struggles of poverty. Some of us were well-provided for, yet we rebelled against our parents. Whatever our problems were, they didn't just materialize from nothing. A seed was planted many years ago that eventually grew into our current dilemmas.

Children are innocent and very vulnerable. They come into this world with a peaceful, open mind. Have you ever watched young children play in the park together? They embrace each other with no cares of race, color, or creed. In their eyes, everyone is equal. It is when they are taught by someone to be prejudiced or unkind that children develop these wrong mindsets. Children adapt to the lifestyles and habits of those around them. They build walls around their hearts to insure that they will be protected. These walls are equivalent to the masks we spoke about earlier in this chapter. Often, when love is lacking in childhood, a child finds it hard to show love. The child becomes an adult who hardens and can become ruthless, feeling, "Life sucks, and nobody really loves me, so I'm not going to love them either."

Some of us suffered abuse, without realizing that what we experienced was abuse, and not realizing how these events negatively influenced our lives. Wrong thinking patterns can be difficult to detect, especially when they are considered normal by those around us. To many, abuse and neglect are commonplace or acceptable. For example, many people raised their children by practicing "tough love." They love their children, yet they don't know how to express it. They were raised by their parents in a similar manner, so they simply adopted tradition and treated their children the same way. As a result, the child grows up feeling unloved, and begins to search for that missing love in other people, places and things, causing a spiral of despair in that child's life. The cycle continues to be passed down from generation to generation until someone in the family takes a stand and breaks the cycle. If this has been the generational cycle in your family, be the one to change, be the one to break it! Disassemble the negative thinking and behavior patterns, teach your children good habits, and don't be afraid to show them love, care, and compassion.

When we begin to recognize the negative influences that have influenced our lives, we open our consciousness and are able to transform our impaired thinking. This step marks the beginning of healing. We all have wounds from our childhood, whether it is the stigma we developed from being called ugly, fat, or stupid, the lack of love we received from our parents, molestation by a loved one or someone we trusted, betrayal or perhaps ridicule that we would never amount to anything. Whatever negative events occurred in our childhood, those events forged the person we see when we look in the mirror today. Take a moment and review your past.

Child abuse is <u>never</u> a child's fault. It is the enemy's trap to defile that child's future. This should not become our excuse to stay as we are, crippled emotionally. We need to recognize the enemy's plan, remove the defilement, and continue to move forward. Circumstances may have influenced our behavior, but those circumstances should not be an excuse to remain stagnant in life. We must actively overcome our barriers by conquering our negative emotions and destroying our "stinking thinking." Each one of us has wounds that need to heal. We cannot heal until we remove our self-made bandages and deal with the root cause of our impairments. Our bandages include toughness, anger, and defiance that we use to cover up our pain. We've had the walls up for years to protect us and to enable us to hide our vulnerabilities. When we realize our inner wounds and their causes, we can clearly identify the reasons for our actions and behavior. Then, the root cause of our problems will quickly come to the surface.

Think about your childhood experiences. Did you receive the love, care, and the compassion you needed? Did you feel safe and secure? Were you ever violated sexually or physically? Did you ever experience verbal abuse? Were both of your parents there to raise you? Did your life turn out to be similar to those who surrounded you as you grew up? These are some of the questions you need to ask yourself to discover the root of your problems.

Often our past wounds cause us to act adversely. Wounded people can act out their pain by becoming insensitive, mean, and rebellious to others. Wounded people often continue the cycle by hurting other people. Their negative patterns become deeply embedded as automatic reactions to the people and circumstances that surround them. Often the meaner and more abusive a person is, the more wounded and abused they were as a child. A person's life often becomes the result of their accumulated experiences. A child who is ridiculed and abused internalizes that treatment. When the child becomes an adult, she doesn't need others to tell her that she's bad, stupid, dumb, a whore, or a thug. She has already begun to adopt the attributes that she was programmed by her parent(s) or others to believe. This programmed belief is "stinking thinking," and it has ruined the lives of many people!

When children grow up in environments that don't empower them, they develop a false self. They use this false self to survive, and they become disconnected from their true self. It is not until we find a safe place where we can share the truths of our pain that we begin to heal. During this process of healing, we can learn to recognize and then dismantle our unproductive, false beliefs. We can then uncover the truth of who we really are. It is important to understand that we cannot bury the past and not address it. The secrets that we hide keep us attached to the shame that the secrets create. When we expose our issues with someone we trust, we break the bondage of shame, we become relieved, and we are able to heal.

Let go of what happened in your childhood. It wasn't your fault! You could not control the events that took place, so forgive yourself. Recognize the plan of the enemy, and release the negative baggage you picked up along the way. You don't have to stay trapped by your past. God is a Healer. He can restore you in every place that you hurt. God's desire is to heal you and make you whole. It is not a coincidence that you are reading this book. You are experiencing a divine appointment. You had to be enlightened to an understanding of your past influences, so you can move victoriously into the future! The future holds many great things for you. Hold on!

We discussed childhood circumstances that altered our true self. Now let's get to know who we really are. Let's awaken together to our true "self."

Many of us have been highly influenced by our surroundings and have adapted to our environment. We have become chameleons, developing personalities that mimic those around us. Not knowing who we are causes us major frustrations. It creates an inner void that we are unable to fill. Our entire existence becomes a lie. We ultimately create the mask of a false self. Incarceration gives us the time we need to evaluate ourselves, to learn what satisfies us, and to understand what truly makes us happy. We can use this time wisely by learning how to love and care for "self." These are the ingredients we need to nurture to create a sense of self-worth. Incarceration takes us from the people, places, and things that we were using as a temporary solution or gratification to cover our inner wounds. Without these distractions, we can clearly see and deal with who and what we really are. Our new environment can allow us to focus on what is most important, the improvement of "self."

The biggest delusion in life is the thought that happiness can be found in external things. This is simply not true. Happiness can only be found within. This is one reason so many marriages and relationships fail. We depend too heavily on others to satisfy our emotional needs. When we are not whole we cannot expect to maintain a healthy relationship with others. Relationships with others cannot complete us. We are completed from within. When we learn how to satisfy our own emotional needs, then we become content in almost any situation or circumstance. Regardless of our conditions or surroundings, we are able to tap into "self" and sustain ourselves through our inner joy.

It is important to use this time to consider what makes us happy. How do you currently feel about yourself? Why? What can you do to improve yourself? How difficult will this be to accomplish? How do you treat others? Would you like others to treat you that way? How strong are the relationships you have developed with others? Are these positive relationships? What do you like to do in your spare time? Are these activities productive? What other productive activities do you think you should start? What are your goals in life? What steps will it take to achieve them? What is your greatest achievement? How did you feel when you accomplished this achievement? What other great achievements will you strive for in the future? These are essential questions you need to ask yourself and to answer thoughtfully and sincerely. Throughout this series we will prepare ourselves for the future by addressing these questions. When we prepare for success and develop a quality plan of action, we gain a new sense of purpose and self-worth. When we are able to examine those areas in our lives where we need improvement and move towards our goals, our sense of well-being increases. Our past adverse circumstances have depleted our self-esteem. When we change our perspective and outlook on life and become happy with ourselves, we will lose our feelings of low self-esteem and replace those feelings with self-confidence. This is our objective during this journey.

When we do not operate in the fullness of who we were created to be, we live in dread and mediocrity. By developing our skill sets and talents within, we can experience a level of success that we previously couldn't imagine! There is greatness inside each of us; it is up to us to find it!

We cannot allow our circumstances to dictate our true identity and our future. We cannot wallow in dysfunction and shame. We must develop the inner strength and determination to cleanse ourselves from life's degradation and move forward, keeping our eyes on the prize! We change our circumstances by changing our thinking. What are you thinking about? What is your focus? In order to be successful, we must train our minds to stay focused on positive things. We have to cut off negative conversations. We don't have time for bickering and gossiping. It's time to become goal-oriented. We must engage in productive activities that promote our growth and development. When we become consumed with positive and productive thinking, we ignite the flame of our inner strength, making us feel happy and energized about "self." It feels good to feel good about "self." It is the power of these positive feelings that motivates us to produce our very best.

It is time to reprogram our thinking. Our thoughts produce our reality. Our job is to reprogram our "stinking thinking." We must let go of our negative patterns from the past and develop new healthy patterns, this begins with our positive thinking and a willingness to change yesterday's experiences, but we can influence our "here and now" experiences. Our present decisions have the power to dictate our future experiences.

A common issue among female inmates that demands our examination is codependency. Many of us don't feel whole by ourselves, so we depend on the companionship of another person to give us a sense of self-worth. A person with low self-esteem usually attracts another troubled person. Together their relationship becomes unhealthy and chaotic. Two incomplete people cannot come together and make each other whole. Each individual will draw on the others' insecurities and that dynamic will eventually destroy the relationship.

Many of us have issues with codependency but they have remained undetected in our consciousness. I was one of those people. I didn't truly understand what codependency was until I read Melody Beattie's, *Codependent No More*. If you discover you may be dealing with codependency issues, I recommend you read this book.

According to Melody Beattie, a codependent person is one who lets another person's behavior affect her, and who is obsessed with controlling that person's behavior. The other person could be a child, an adult, a lover, a spouse, a brother, a sister, a grandparent, a client, or a best friend.

Often when a codependent person discontinues her relationship with a troubled individual, she seeks another troubled person and continues the cycle. A common denominator of codependents is to have relationships, personally or professionally, with troubled, needy, or other dependent people.

Codependent behavior is self-destructive. In these relationships we react to people who are destroying themselves. We react to them by destroying ourselves. This behavior keeps us trapped in negative, disruptive relationships and compels us to ruin relationships that might otherwise have worked. A codependent person is constantly manipulating circumstances to control the actions of their partner. "If I do this, it will cause him to stay home." "If I give her that, I know she won't go anywhere." We get trapped in the rut of manipulating people to act the way we want them to act. Our effort to manipulate ultimately fails, even if it worked temporarily. Nobody wants to be manipulated or controlled. When a person finally understands that they have been manipulated, they will become angry and rebel. The relationship becomes a series of destructive behaviors, with one inflicted wound following another. It is critical to understand this one valuable lesson: WE CANNOT CHANGE PEOPLE! The only person we can control is our self. All our efforts to change other people will fail! Change can only occur when a person makes the choice to change! Nothing you do can alter this fact!

Codependency is the dependency on people, their moods, behaviors, sicknesses or well-being, and their love for us, to make us happy. Codependents appear to be dependable and very strong on the outside, yet inside they feel helpless. We appear at first to be controlling, but we are really the ones who are being controlled by the people we are codependent on. We become attached, and at times obsessive, and believe that we need these people in our lives in order to be fulfilled. This unhealthy attachment causes us to overreact to the person's emotions and behavior. We may become caretakers, rescuers, or enablers to them, attaching ourselves to their need for us. Our thought process becomes: "They need me." This need gives us a false sense of self-worth. As a result, we dedicate our lives to meeting the needs of that person. Our low self-esteem makes us vulnerable to this "needy" person. We believe our importance is established because we are so important to them. As a result we consume ourselves with taking care of others. Think: are these behavior patterns familiar to you and evidenced in your relationships?

When we focus all our energy on other people and their problems, we have little or no time left to care for ourselves. In the end, we neglect our own needs, and deep down, we remain empty and miserable. Our partners, on the other hand, become carefree. We become overworked, and they remain relaxed. Typically in codependent relationships, codependents take care of other people's responsibilities and then later, they become angry at themselves for doing so. They begin to feel used and sorry for themselves, causing them to inflict pain upon their partners. A codependent person moves from being a rescuer to a victim, to a manipulator.

When we become obsessed with people and their needs, we become unaware of our own feelings because our focus is on others and their issues. We begin to resent the other person, so we start to persecute the person we are codependent on. We bring up things we've done for them, and lash out when they don't act the way we feel they should. Then, the other person returns the attack and our fear of living without that person keeps us entangled in the destructive web, only to repeat the cycle of caretaking to sustain the relationship. Life becomes a chaotic nightmare, with constant bickering and fighting as the result. Even still, we maintain the false hope that things will get better and <u>our</u> needs will be met one day, yet that day never comes.

The only solution to codependency is detachment. It may be frightening at first, because we are forced to confront the fear of being alone and acknowledge emotions we may not be ready to face. Detachment, in the end, is worth it! It is better for everyone involved. Detachment does not have to be a cold, hostile withdrawal, nor does it have to be the removal of our love or concern for a person. Detachment is an act of love for ourselves; it is a "time-out" that we so desperately need to allow ourselves to become whole. We gain release from a person or a problem that is unhealthy for us and the release gives us a chance to reexamine ourselves. Detachment is based on the premise that each person is responsible for him- or herself. We shouldn't try to solve problems that aren't ours to solve. We do not have the ability to control or change another person. We can only control and change ourselves. Detachment begins our journey of caring for "self." We then are able to become focused on our own emotional needs and weaknesses. When we don't care for "self" and allow "self" to be disrespected, we send a message that others should not respect us either. When we develop love, care, and respect for "self," others will respect us as well.

Self-respect starts with boundaries. We must learn to draw the line of what we will and will not tolerate. We have the power to set our own boundaries! When we enter relationships, we are able to create the parameters for the relationship. Always remember, how you allow a relationship to begin is the same way it will end. If you tolerate disrespect, you will be shown disrespect throughout the entire course of the relationship. Take hold of your power from the beginning, and never allow anyone to mistreat you. Nip abuse in the bud by detaching yourself immediately. Do not give in! Let your "yes" be "yes" and your "no" be "no." When people see how strongly you respect yourself, they will either have great respect for you, or they will leave. If a person decides to leave, it is okay. We must learn to trust God, that He alone is our Provider, not other people. Just as a disrespectful person came into your life, God can send you a person who will respect you. Never replace God with a person. Do not allow a person to manipulate your emotions. If you do you will have prioritized that person above yourself. How dangerous! Do not give another person that power over you. Be willing to walk away.

Other people do not ultimately have the ability to change who we are. However, we can allow them to influence us. Just because people may have manipulated us or done us wrong in the past, we do not need to become uncompassionate. We must release all negativity from our lives, including negative people. When people adversely affect our happiness, that's when we must make the choice to detach. The moment we release these individuals is the moment of our greatest miracle. Often, when we begin to care for "self," those around us are also able to heal, and, by our example, they become better equipped to function positively. People do not have to grow up if someone is always rescuing them. When forced to care for themselves, they often are forced to develop healthy emotions. Often we think we are "enabling" people with our help but, in reality, we are "disabling" them, since they do not learn to care for themselves. We must learn to remove our hands from God's work! Let Him mold people into who He wants them to become. The bottom line is to learn to care for "self."

In the beginning of a stormy season, it is common to wonder why God is allowing these circumstances. We begin to feel sad, hopeless, and depressed because we feel unloved. It is as though we are being punished, but the truth is that we are being honored. We are special to God. God chastens or corrects those whom He loves. Trials and tribulations strengthen us. God knows that if we are challenged, we will grow in our development. He doesn't want us to stay stuck in the same old patterns that will only lead to self-destruction. God's will is for us to obtain victory in our lives. Therefore, if we are headed down the wrong road, He will allow turbulence to occur. It is His way of getting our attention and alerting us that there are problems we need to fix.

Adversity reveals our true character. Difficult times allow us to see what we are made of. When we are tested and tried, our hearts are exposed. Crisis does not have to be a bad thing. We can transform it into a gift of opportunity to change. We now have the chance to work on "self." We become true "overcomers" when we are able to overcome adversity!

Our perceived crisis has now led us to a new journey called "self-discovery." When we are aligned with our "self," we naturally experience greater wisdom, compassion, and love as we begin to heal. We become aware of our fundamental inner goodness from which many of us have been disconnected because of "stinking thinking." This series will take us step by step through our healing process.

Healing exposes who we really are. In the process of restoring our consciousness to correct reality, we eliminate false deceptions of who we *thought* we were. Healing includes taking back what belongs to us emotionally, emerging from denial, and being fully restored. We cannot complete this process until we are honest about our past mistakes. Healing requires us to examine the parts of our lives that we have locked away and hidden deep down inside. It takes courage to do this, because when we become honest about ourselves, we expose our inner fears, pain, and feelings of worthlessness that are at the root of our criminal behavior. Healing requires getting to the root of the problem, recognizing it, and then destroying it. This circumspection is discovering our true beauty within and learning how to appreciate and love ourselves.

Now that we have evaluated the root of many of our problems, it is time to repair ourselves. Let's begin our journey of healing! This process is different for each person. It may be painful and very emotional at times, but do not quit. The results are well worth it. Take your time and go through each of the chapters thoroughly. Each chapter will bring about another phase of restoration. Each stage will allow you to receive solutions to the various problems you have encountered throughout life. Study and consider the information, then apply it to your own experiences.

Let's close this chapter with a prayer: *"God, I thank You for coming into my life and revealing to me some of the roots of my problems. I ask that You daily reveal to me my shortcomings and grant me the strength and ability to correct them. Help me to become aware of 'self' and guide me through this process of healing. Give me insight to my problems and provide me with divine solutions. Cleanse my heart and mind of all defilement and prepare me for this journey. Empower me to remain honest and open throughout this process. Help me to completely heal and allow me to be made whole. Amen."*

You are now officially on the road to restoration. Stay focused and persistent along this journey. Good luck - you can do it!

CHAPTER QUESTIONS
1) Why are many of us not happy with ourselves?
2) Why is it easy to get caught up in a false identity of "self?"
3) How do childhood experiences affect who we are today?
4) Why are children easily influenced?

5) What is codependency?

WRITING ASSIGNMENT

In your journal, write out an assessment of your childhood. List significant events in your life; describe how they made you feel at the time, and how they ultimately affected your life. Provide details.

CHAPTER 4

Acknowledging Our Shortcomings

In the last chapter, we discussed some of the main roots of our problems. We learned that many of us have been wearing a mask, assuming the identity of a false "self," and that we have worn these masks so long that it is hard to differentiate between our real "self" and this illusionary one. Now it is time to focus on our reality. We cannot heal until we take off these masks and reveal our shortcomings. This process can be very uncomfortable and at times painful, because exposing our imperfections uncovers our areas of vulnerability. Few people are willing to admit their mistakes and downfalls, so they take the easy way out, they hide their weaknesses. It's so much easier to blame others for our problems than to take responsibility for our own actions and enact change. The longer we hide our problems, the longer we stay stagnant. True healing will not occur until we are willing to be honest with ourselves. We must honestly evaluate our lives and our wrong behavioral patterns. If not, we will remain slaves to destructive life patterns.

Denial is deadly! It creates dishonesty, manipulation, paralysis, fear and feelings of inadequacy. It is the trap that keeps us locked behind the prison doors of our souls. Denial is also torment! In order to suppress the truth, we live a substandard existence full of lies. Our attempts to hide the truth cause us to experience unnecessary pain on a continuous basis because we have no means of release. Freedom only occurs when we expose the truth.

When we are in denial, we attempt to cover up our wounds with self-made bandages; we build up walls of protection around our hearts and souls, which stops us from getting to the core of our problems. These blocking devices create new weaknesses that in turn continue the cycle of deception, covering up the real issues. Mired in denial, we eventually self-destruct. Locked behind the lonely doors of grief, our inner spirit never has a chance to heal.

Many of us choose to stay in denial because we are afraid of what others may think about us. The fear of being misunderstood, and possibly losing the love of others, keeps us concealed behind the doors of denial. We believe that if we expose our inner truth, people will no longer view us the same way, and they will develop a different opinion of us based on their new discoveries. This fear causes us to keep our mask on tightly. We assume a false identity and live it as if it is our own, hiding the truth of who we really are.

In this chapter, we are going to begin our healing process by exposing the truth. We are in this place, at this time, for a reason! Whether it be the punishment for a crime we have committed or an enlightenment to change some incorrect behavior patterns, we are here in this season, at this time, to work on "self." To heal, we must be honest with ourselves about the mistakes we made in the past, without beating ourselves up for making them. We cannot change what has happened in the past, but we can recognize our errors and learn from them. It's okay that we made mistakes. Everyone makes them, but some mistakes have greater consequences than others. Examining our mistakes, whether big or small, allows us to grow. There is no success without failure! Failure occurs so we can learn from our experiences. Failures are the training wheels we use to develop the skills we need to ride smoothly through life. Just as we dispose of our training wheels as we develop balance when we learn to ride a bike, we must also dispose the reproach of our past. We learn from the experiences, and then we move on! We begin to mature when we expose our errors, and take off our masks. Don't stay ensnared in a lie! Let's break the chains of denial. This gives us the room we need to grow.

This process of healing is going to require us to journey down memory lane and pinpoint where we made our errors. When we clearly identify our mistakes, we can deprogram the wrong thinking patterns we assumed and reprogram our minds with correct thinking patterns. When we accurately spotlight the places where we went wrong in our lives and acknowledge our errors, we open the doors to freedom. We no longer have to stay in the bondage of denial. We are then free to be ourselves, and no longer have to lie about who we are. This removes the heavy burdens many of us have been carrying for years.

For some of us, a specific incident or a particular life crisis as a youth or even as an adult preceded us getting into trouble. For example, the death of a loved one, the separation from a parent because of divorce, molestation, or some other event of loss or abuse may have sparked negative behavioral cycles in our lives. It is important that we acknowledge these events and deal with them emotionally, so that we won't stay trapped by them. When we are able to distinguish where we went wrong and why, we are clearly able to visualize how we were influenced by the initial problem.

This revelation allows us to see that we have become a product of our environment or a result of circumstances. Our lives have become what they are today based on a series of events that caused our thinking patterns to become distorted. When we truly understand this concept, we are able to grasp the keys needed to unlock the doors of denial. We can then accept responsibility and move forward positively, by correcting our thinking patterns. The problems we thought had no solutions are given a resolution. We become relieved as we discover that we are not crazy or hopeless, as many of us have been told. We were infected by "stinking thinking" passed down to us from others who influenced our lifestyles. Now we will cure ourselves by changing our incorrect mindset. First, we discover the problem. Then, we activate the cure!

Prison for many of us has been a challenging experience. There is little to hide behind in prison: no people, no places, and no things! Surrounded by strangers, we are forced to deal with our issues head-on. Each day we wake up, locked behind prison walls, forced to deal with, in our minds, the cause of why we are here. Most people take the easy way out and blame someone else for their incarceration. The common thought is, "I'm here because of such and such." "If they wouldn't have done that to me, I wouldn't be here." Very few people have the courage to admit that they were wrong in their actions and that their poor choices landed them in prison. When we don't accept responsibility, we stay enmeshed in the deception of denial. We cover ourselves with a new mask and begin to take on another false identity. Again, healing cannot occur until we remove our masks!

Let's take an honest look at the events that led up to our incarceration. Each of us somewhere down the line made a poor choice. Whether it was actually committing an illegal act ourselves or being around someone else who did something illegal, we all made a mistake. Our wrong choices and associations allowed us to fall prey to our current situation. It was the decision to make ourselves vulnerable to be apprehended by law enforcement that brought us to this point. Had we not been in that particular place, around those people we associated with, we would not be in prison! There are very few instances that negate this truth, such as being falsely identified, but generally it was our faulty reasoning in choices that led us to imprisonment. Many of us don't want to accept this fact, but it is the truth. And it's the truth that will set us free! In order to move forward we have to accept our shortcomings. It is destructive to continue placing blame on everyone else except ourselves. It's time to grow up and be real women! In order to mature emotionally, we must be willing to take responsibility for our actions.

Accepting responsibility brings about a release. It unhooks us from the trap of denial and allows us to correct our vision, so that we can successfully move through life. Acceptance is the secret ingredient that enables change to occur. It brings peace and contentment, which allow us to grow in healthy emotions. Accepting responsibility finally puts us in position to discover what we need to do to take care of ourselves, and improve our lives. Acceptance is empowerment! It is our confession to God that we are finally ready to surrender and allow Him to help us fix our shortcomings.

Along with the healing process of accepting responsibility we must also examine our behavioral patterns that led us down the wrong path of life. This will be a very difficult step for most of us. It is a painful emotional process, but the "pros" far outweigh the "cons." Let's use the next part of this journey to honestly assess some of our weaknesses. This inventory will allow us to understand the wrong mindsets we have developed and must change. It is important that we accurately assess our areas of weaknesses and vulnerability, so that we can strengthen and improve them. Take the time during this section to open up your memory to the actions of your past that may have exhibited these tendencies.

The process of taking a fearless moral inventory of ourselves is also Step 4 in the Alcoholics Anonymous program. The purpose of this inventory is to sort through the confusion and the contradictions of our lives, in order to discover who we truly are. It helps to rid us of the burdens and traps that controlled the thinking that prevented our growth.

Writing down our inventory helps us to overcome the obstacles of self-deception and rationalization. It unlocks the portion of our subconscious mind that has been concealing the truth of who we are. When we start this step, we let go of fear by simply putting our thoughts on paper. Writing out our inventory helps us to be done with our past and no longer bound by it. It gives us the courage to look our past in the face, see it for what it really is, discard it, and move on.

Now it's time to get in touch with your "self." Take out your *Voices of Consequences, "Unlocking the Prison Doors"* Workbook/Journal. Complete the Moral Inventory List of Weaknesses, in Chapter 4 of the Workbook/Journal. The activities will help you identify and discard any layers of false identities. Write about your liabilities, such as guilt, shame, remorse, self-pity, resentment, anger, depression, frustration, confusion, loneliness, anxiety, betrayal, hopelessness, failure, fear, and denial. Go through the exercises in the journal, take the time you need to assess and complete them, and then turn back to this chapter. You will be amazed by your discoveries!

A fearless moral inventory helps us to examine our weaknesses, which led us to commit acts of the flesh. We cannot sustain peace when we operate in these areas of unethical behavior. They include adultery, fornication, unclean actions, lewdness, idolatry, sorcery, hatred, contentions, jealousies, outbursts of wrath, selfish ambitions, dissensions, heresies, envy, murders, drunkenness, revelries, and the like. These forbidden acts are introduced to us in the Bible, in Galatians, Chapter 5, verses 19-21. We must make a conscious effort to acknowledge the areas in which we have acted poorly in our past. The consequences of these behavioral patterns are fatal. You cannot maintain a healthy life while practicing them! The outcome will always be failure, and if you refuse to change, the final outcome is self-destruction. The price to pay for the temporary pleasures they bring is simply not worth it! Recognize and then uproot these negative behavior patterns.

We are all God's wonderful creations. There is goodness in each one of us. It is our job to find that goodness within and express it. When we recognize our good characteristics we will see a clear, accurate picture of our true "self." These characteristics include being open-minded, honest, generous, kind, caring, courageous, faithful, clean, grateful, loving, joyous, peaceful, patient, gentle, and self-controlled. When we operate using these characteristics, we operate according to the Spirit of God, which is God's plan for our lives. These characteristics are introduced in the Bible, in Galatians, Chapter 5, verses 22-23. They are considered the fruits of the Spirit.

In the *Voice of Consequences, "Unlocking the Prison Doors"* Workbook/Journal, take an assessment of your strengths. Complete the Moral Inventory of Good Character Traits, located in Chapter 4 of your Workbook/Journal. Do the exercises that are listed, and then return to this chapter.

Now that you have discovered your strengths and your weaknesses, you have unveiled your true "self." You can now move forward successfully, because you have a clear picture of who you really are. Now it is our job to discard all our weaknesses and increase our strengths. Practice daily expressing the fruits of your strengths. The stress once trapped inside is now released, and you are free to be your true "self," which is the person God created you to be.

The next section of this chapter will deal with wrong associations and unhealthy relationships. Many of us are in our current position because of our associations with negative people! In order to be productive, we must surround ourselves with positive people. These are people who believe in us, who share our values, and who uplift and encourage us. Anyone that doesn't express these attributes toward us should not be accepted in our immediate circles.

Negative people contaminate us with their "stinking thinking" and wrong mindsets. They drain us of positive energy and take away our focus. Many of us have allowed our lives to be consumed with a continual cycle of bad associations, which have inevitably influenced our actions. Today it's time to recognize these negative relationships and remove them from our lives!

In the *Voices of Consequences, "Unlocking the Prison Doors"* Workbook/Journal, complete the Bad Relationships Inventory List located in Chapter 4. Do the exercises in that section as well as complete the inventory list, then return to reading this chapter.

The Bad Relationships Inventory has helped us identify the relationships in our lives that we need to sever. This is a very important step! People are very influential, and their habits can become contagious. If we allow ourselves to spend too much time with negative people, they can contaminate us with their "stinking thinking." We should be extremely careful of those whom we allow into our inner circle. Don't allow people to dump their trash in your backyard! Put them off your premises, and sever all ties!

A good way to evaluate a person, to determine if his or her friendship is a good association for you, is by asking them where they are in life and where they are going. This question exposes a person's intent and direction in life. If they are not headed down the same path as you wish to go, cut them loose! If you don't, they can potentially destroy your plans. Take time to listen to the conversations this person has with others. Are these conversations positive? Does this person talk about productive things? If not, you shouldn't be around their idle talk. It's senseless and a waste of your time! What we allow ourselves to hear begins to quickly seep into our spirits, and we take on those negative thought patterns. Soon we will find ourselves doing the same things we heard being discussed. Influence starts with idle talk. What idle talk have you taken part in lately?

Good relationships are created by the support and strength they bring us. They are made with people who encourage us to become our best. These people live their lives by example doing productive things, and they encourage us to do the same. Who do you currently have in your life that possesses these attributes? These people are gifts from God; keep them close and honor their friendship!

Many of the people we have associated with in our past have hidden intentions. The truth is these people do not want to see our success. The statement "misery loves company" is so true! Many who have been unable to achieve success don't want to see us achieve it either. These people are called our "haters" or "secret enemies." They smile to our faces and entertain us as friends, yet they secretly pray for our downfall. These people are not happy with themselves, and in many ways, they are jealous of us, even though we haven't reached our maximum potential. Subconsciously they recognize our potential. They are frightened that we will recognize who we can become and surpass them, so they strive to keep us down by using tactics to decrease our confidence. They divert us from our focus and encourage destructive behavior. If we stay in these bad associations, they will ultimately delay our success. Who are the "secret enemies" in your life? Do you recognize these traits in any of your so-called friends? Now that you know who they are, get rid of them!

Let's travel on this journey baggage-free! It will make our trip so much easier. Put closure to all unhealthy relationships, and walk away in peace. If we choose to let our past trap us, then we cannot move into the future. There are no exceptions to the rule! All negative people have an adverse effect on our lives. We many not recognize it at first but, sooner or later, they will contaminate us with their negative energy.

Letting people go whom we love can be difficult. Many of us believe in our hearts we cannot live without certain people in our lives. This is not true! When we let go of unhealthy relationships, the lights turn on for us. Suddenly we are able to see clearly. To let them go does not mean we no longer love them, it just means that, at this point in our lives, we love ourselves more. Our new love for "self" no longer allows negative relationships to destroy us. We take responsibility for our choices, and we choose positive, productive people to become a part of our inner circle.

We have acknowledged our weaknesses, strengths, wrong associations, and positive relationships present in our life. Now it's time to address our crimes and the behavior patterns that led us to our incarceration. Many of us have not honestly examined our actions, nor assessed the effects that our behavior has had on others. This is very selfish. It is important that we truly realize that our behaviors were wrong. Until we accept that fact, we will never change and move forward in life. If we keep the doors open to criminal thinking, we will ultimately be led down the path of self-destruction, which ends with death. We must understand that until we recognize our actions as being incorrect, we will not change them.

Life isn't over! We can be successful without illegal activities. Most criminals have great minds, which is how we are able to put together and pull off massive schemes. Now it's time to use these minds productively. We can have just as much success legitimately, and even greater, and we can sustain it with peace of mind, joy and happiness. We achieve this by working on developing our skill sets and talents. As we do, we will be able to set up legal avenues of income and recognition. This will enable us to achieve major successes in life.

No one gets away with crime! It will eventually catch up with us. Avoid the headache and take the needed steps to build a healthy, prosperous, law-abiding life. We cannot get to this step until we realize that what we have been doing is wrong. Scrutinize your life and take a good look at the events that led up to your incarceration. Sincerely ask yourself the question, "What did I do wrong?" Recap all your actions that were unethical. What could you have done differently? Ponder these thoughts.

Congratulations! It took a lot of courage to get us to this point. Even after you complete the exercises in this chapter, you may discover additional events and adverse behavioral patterns that you need to adjust. Make it an ongoing process to continually take an inventory of your weaknesses. As you allow these traits to come to the surface and examine them, you can consciously change your behavior. The choice is yours. You have the power to become the best person you can be, but this takes work! We must constantly re-examine ourselves. It is our awareness that brings about correct solutions.

Let's close this chapter with a prayer: *"God, I thank You for the strength to expose my shortcomings. I understand that if I am unable to recognize my faults, I will also be unable to fix them. Help me to see myself through Your eyes. Daily show me the characteristics You wish me to change. Let me know when I fall short of Your standards. Gently nudge me and guide me back into the correct direction. I now ask for the strength I need to travel through this journey of restoration. Heal me and make me whole. Amen."*

CHAPTER QUESTIONS

1) Why is denial dangerous?
2) Why do bad character traits cause stagnation in our lives?
3) List some bad character traits.
4) List some good character traits.
5) Why is it dangerous to associate with negative people?

WRITING ASSIGNMENT

Write a list of all the personal weaknesses you have discovered while completing your moral inventory. Discuss how each of these characteristics led to your imprisonment. Detail what negative behavioral patterns you developed as a result of each weakness. Explain how you will improve your overall "self" in order not to repeat the same mistakes.

CHAPTER 5

Accepting Responsibility for Our Actions

I n the last chapter, we explored our shortcomings and
acknowledged our wrong behaviors. We learned that in order
to receive restoration, we must expose the truth of our past.
Now that the truth has been revealed, we must go a step further.
In this chapter, we will prepare ourselves to be willing and able to
accept responsibility for our actions. This is a vital prerequisite
to restoration.

Acknowledging our shortcomings and accepting responsibility are two very different steps. Acknowledging our faults is
allowing ourselves to understand what we did wrong. Accepting
responsibility for our actions is the act of feeling remorse for our
wrongdoings, and changing our course of action. We cannot
become remorseful until we fully understand the effects our
behavior has had on others. In this chapter, we will explore the
impact our crimes have had on our victims.

Have you ever taken the time to really analyze the lives
your crime has affected? How do you think your victims feel?
Who have you hurt by committing your crime, besides yourself?
In this section, we will take a look at the lives that have been
adversely affected by our crimes. For some of us, this will be
the first time that we truly understand the pain we have caused

others. The goal of this chapter is for each of us to recognize the overall effects of our crimes, allowing us to become remorseful for our actions.

We all are in prison for different crimes, from petty theft to murder. Regardless of the crime, our actions have adversely affected other individuals besides ourselves. Today we will examine our crimes from a victim's standpoint. I will share with you three stories that represent three different types of crimes, and illustrate the impact on each victim.

EXAMPLE #1: MARIA

Maria's childhood was one of struggle, in a New York City housing project. Growing up there was difficult for Maria and her siblings. She never met her father, and her mother was very sickly. Her mother was always going in and out of the hospital. There were many nights that Maria had very little to eat. At times, there was no food at all to feed her brothers and sisters, so Maria decided to take matters into her own hands. Maria met Juan, who was a local drug dealer from her building, and she shared her problems with him. Juan offered Maria what she thought at the time was a viable solution. He told Maria that if she was willing to go to Mexico and pick up some drugs to bring back to the U.S., she could make a lot of money. Believing this was an adequate solution to her dilemma; Maria accepted the offer and began transporting drugs. For over a year, every two months or so, Maria would bring back a massive amount of drugs from Mexico to the U.S.

Life quickly improved for Maria. She had more money than she knew what to do with! She showered her family with gifts, and even moved her mother out of the rundown housing projects. Life was good. Maria didn't have a care in the world, or so she thought. Trafficking drugs was accredited as the solution to her life's obstacles.

Life was good, until one day when Maria's cousin asked Maria to buy her a cell phone. Maria chose not to buy her cousin the phone because she felt her cousin didn't need it. Maria had helped this cousin on numerous occasions. She had recently given her cousin the money to move into her own apartment. Maria also had bought her cousin a car to transport her children back and forth to school. However, Maria said "no" to the cell phone request, and never thought about it further. Filled with jealousy and anger, Maria's cousin called the cops and tipped them off to Maria's next trip to Mexico.

Caught off guard, Maria was stopped at customs for what she thought was a random check. She had her drugs well stashed so she wasn't too concerned. It took her by surprise when the customs agents pulled Maria in the office, and they told her to remove the drugs. They knew exactly where the drugs were hidden! Maria knew at that point she was set up. She wept profusely as she realized she was in deep trouble!

After sitting in the county jail for several months, facing federal charges with a 10-year mandatory minimum sentence, Maria received her discovery paperwork from her lawyer, which revealed her snitch. To her surprise, it was the cousin she had helped support with the money she made trafficking drugs. Maria felt hurt, betrayed, and devastated. To top it off, her mom couldn't afford the home that Maria had bought her, so Maria's family landed on the streets, forced to move in with relatives. Maria became suicidal. In the county jail, she had a nervous breakdown and was moved to the medical ward. In the medical ward, Maria met a lady who helped change Maria's entire life.

While Maria rested in bed severely depressed, she met a woman by the name of Sandra, who lived in the same housing project as Maria. Sandra's bed was next to Maria's. She began to pray with Maria daily and read her Bible stories. Sandra brought life back to Maria. They would talk and share stories with each other for many hours. Maria discovered Sandra also knew Juan, the same man who had convinced Maria to transport drugs. Sandra was a heroin addict who was diagnosed with full-blown AIDS. She had been struggling with her sickness for quite some time and was told by the doctors, in the medical ward, that she had less than six months to live. As Maria's health quickly began to get better, Sandra's health began to decline.

One day Sandra told Maria how Juan had introduced her to heroin. Both Sandra and Juan were young teens who partied a lot. During their era, coke was the "in thing" to do, so they both started sniffing coke. Eventually, Sandra's body became immune to coke, so Juan began feeding Sandra heroin - she got hooked. Sandra told Maria how she lied, cheated, stole, and even sold her body to support her addiction. She was so strung out that she lost everything, including her two children to Child Services. She had another baby a year ago, who was born mentally disabled and HIV positive. Just ten days after he was born, Sandra's son died. Sandra became severely depressed and sought more drugs to take away her pain. Along with heroin, she also abused prescription drugs. In desperation she borrowed a gun and attempted to hold up the local pharmacy, where she was disarmed by the store manager, who held her until the police came. She was now awaiting her sentencing for the armed robbery charge.

During the several days the women spent in the county medical ward together, they became very close. Maria began to take care of Sandra just as Sandra took care of her. Maria watched Sandra deteriorate before her eyes. She stayed by Sandra's side as Sandra moaned from pain at night. One day Sandra told Maria how she had not spoken to her mother in six years. She cried as she explained how she stole her mother's rent money to support her drug habit, almost causing her to be evicted. Her mother, finally fed up, severed all ties. Maria convinced Sandra to reach out to her mother. Sandra called her mom, who was happy to hear from her, and her mother came to the ward to visit Sandra. Maria watched the tears stream down the face of the mother and daughter, and she also began to cry. Maria had never thought before how the drugs she had transported affected others. She only thought about her gain. She had never taken the time to consider the family members who would suffer because of the addiction of their loved ones, the children it would hurt, and the mothers who would bury their children. These worries began to run through Maria's head. It all became a reality to Maria as she slept next to one of her victims in the medical ward. She realized that drugs she had transported from Mexico were sold to Sandra, inflicting the pain she'd witnessed. At that moment, her perception of her crime began to change. She became truly remorseful and fully realized the effects of her illegal activity.

EXAMPLE #2 – KEISHA

Keisha grew up in a middle-class family in Englewood, N.J. Keisha lived a very good life. Her parents provided well for her and her siblings. When Keisha turned 16, she started dating a local drug dealer, who spoiled her with a lavish display of fancy gifts, and eventually the two of them moved in together. Keisha quickly fell in love with the money and her boyfriend's lifestyle.

Everything seemed great in Keisha's life, until one early morning when the Feds raided her home and locked her boyfriend up. Keisha felt all alone, as if her life had ended. She moved back in with her parents, but was deeply depressed that she was unable to sustain her previous lifestyle.

Discussing these problems one day with a childhood friend, Ann, Keisha heard what she thought was a solution. Ann was a hustler who committed bank fraud for a living. Ann drove a brand-new Benz, wore designer clothes, and had expensive jewelry. Keisha, looking at Ann's lifestyle, felt as though bank fraud was the way out of her problems. Ann and Keisha became partners, and they started stealing the identities of older people, going into their bank accounts and wiping out their money.

Quickly, Keisha began to see money flowing in, even more than she was accustomed to from her boyfriend, the drug dealer. Keisha bought a new Range Rover and a condo in a high-rise building downtown. Keisha was able to send her children to the best schools, and she lived well for several years. All was well until one day, Ann, Keisha's partner, got caught by the Feds.

Keisha had no clue Ann was ever arrested. Faced with the pressure of doing extensive time in jail, Ann allowed the Feds to wire her, and she began to set up Keisha. She recorded hours of the two of them preparing to defraud the bank. She also introduced Keisha to an undercover agent to conduct business. Keisha, believing Ann was her friend, also discussed with Ann the business of Keisha's new fiancé, Bill, who was a big-time drug dealer. Ann had enough information from Keisha to also set up Bill with a new large customer, who was, of course, a federal agent.

Within a matter of months, the FBI and the DEA raided Keisha and Bill's condo and found 6 kilos of cocaine and 3 handguns stashed inside the walls of the house. Of course, Keisha told Ann about the stash spot, and Ann had tipped off the agents. When the FBI and the DEA apprehended the two with the drugs and the guns from the house, they also immediately took Keisha's children and turned them over to Child Services.

Keisha was charged and held without bail. She was stressed and afraid, especially because of the loss of her children to children's services. Keisha phoned Ann from jail. To her surprise, Ann was very short and uncaring. She told Keisha that she had her own problems, and she hung up. Keisha was hurt and greatly disappointed. She couldn't understand why her friend would abandon her in a time like this. One month later, the story began to make sense. Keisha's lawyer advised her that Ann had set her up and was scheduled to testify against Keisha at her grand jury hearing. Keisha was devastated! She felt hurt, angry, and betrayed. Furthermore, Bill's Columbian drug connection knew Bill was set up by Ann, but the connection also believed Keisha had something to do with it, because for years they observed the closeness between the two women. The Columbian drug dealers began to send threats to Keisha's family members, demanding the drug money. This caused tremendous pressure on Keisha. She felt victimized and wondered why all this was happening to her. Luckily, Keisha's boyfriend took the drug and gun charges and Keisha faced only the identity theft and bank fraud charges.

On her day of sentencing, Keisha went to court, and at the hearing, one of the victims of her identity theft fraud scheme stood up and spoke. The lady was a thirty-nine-year-old, middle-class, white woman from Houston, TX. She had flown in to appear at Keisha's sentencing. As the woman approached the stand, tears began to roll down her cheeks. Keisha wondered, Why is this lady taking this so seriously? The woman spoke softly into the microphone on the court stand and said, "I do," as she was sworn in, and began to tell her story. She explained that she had come from Texas to testify, but that her mother was the actual victim. Her mother was a seventy-eight-year-old woman who worked two jobs most of her life to make ends meet. The woman explained how her mother struggled to support her and her two sisters after their father died in a car accident. The older woman had worked hard to leave something behind for her children. She grew up very poor, and she never wanted her children to experience the poverty that she had. Therefore, she had taken great pride in saving money for her children. One morning the *mother went to the bank to make a deposit only to discover that all of her money was gone from the account. Keisha and Ann had made up phony checks and created a false ID to present to the bank, and they had cleared out the woman's account. The mother was devastated! She felt as though everything she had labored for was gone. Even though the bank assured her that they would get to the bottom of it, anxiety overtook the woman. That night the elderly woman had a heart attack and died.*

As the daughter told the story, Keisha began to cry. She had no idea how her crime could affect another person. She always rationalized that the banks had insurance coverage and that they would replace the victims' money. She never considered what she was doing as wrong; to Keisha it was mere survival! It was at that moment that Keisha changed her perspective of her crime. She felt very sad and remorseful. If she had not cleared out the account, the woman would still be alive.

EXAMPLE #3 – DEBBIE

Debbie grew up in Los Angeles, California in a very poor family. Her mom struggled to care single-handedly for Debbie and her six siblings. Her mom worked three jobs, causing her to rarely have time to spend with her children. Debbie and her siblings practically raised themselves.

Missing the love and attention Debbie craved, she was easily influenced to join a local gang. For the first time in her life, Debbie felt as though she was loved and cared for by her fellow gang members. She vowed to "ride" or "die" with them to the bitter end.

At one of the meetings, it was decided that the gang members would arrange a robbery of one of the local banks. They decided that Debbie would go inside the bank with them as a decoy, but Debbie was reluctant. Something inside kept telling her not to go. At the last minute she decided to back out, and the gang offered her a look-out position instead. She thought that there couldn't be too much harm in waiting outside, so she agreed.

A few days later, Debbie and the gang members headed to the bank to complete the robbery. Everyone was wearing masks and gloves, and they were ready to pull off their heist! Debbie stayed in the car as the look-out. The homies jumped out of the car and ran into the bank. As they went in, Debbie began to patrol the premises. Inside the bank the homies had their guns drawn and tied up the security officer, forcing the bank manager to lead the gang members to the safe. While all this was going on, Debbie spotted a customer who was driving into the parking lot. The customer noticed what was going on through his view of the tall clear bank windows. As he backed out of the lot, the customer used his cell phone to report the robbery. Debbie saw what the man was doing, so she ran into the bank to alert the homies of the possible danger. Debbie was so nervous that as she entered the bank, she made a great commotion. Frightened by her entrance, the homies believed she was the police and they got nervous. The one holding the security officer panicked and let him go. The man broke loose from the rope and reached for his gun. One of the other gang members spotted his actions and shot the officer three times in the head. The bullets instantly killed him! Startled by the gunshots, the homies quickly left the bank. It was too late! The customer in the parking lot had already summoned the police and had given them the license plate number of the gang's car as well as a description of the car. The homies ended up in a high pursuit chase with the cops, which ended in a crash. Two innocent passengers in the car they hit died. All of the perpetrators were apprehended by the police, including Debbie.

What Debbie perceived to be an innocent job as look-out turned into a triple homicide! Debbie was charged with armed robbery and first degree murder, and she was held without bail in the local county jail. She was deeply depressed, realizing she could receive a life sentence. Debbie prayed to God for a solution.

One day Debbie got a visit from the wife of the security officer that was killed in the bank. She told Debbie she couldn't rest until she met Debbie and the other gang members, because she needed to forgive them in order to make peace with God. She was a devout Christian woman who was active in her church. She served God whole-heartedly in her congregation and in her community, but after the death of her husband, she gave up on God. She couldn't understand why God would allow this devastating event to happen to her husband. For months she cried, and she rarely ate or slept. She also lost her job and fell behind in her bills. Her husband had insurance coverage, but it paid out very little, just enough to cover the cost of the funeral arrangements and a few other payments. The woman had no job, and without the income of her husband, she fell into great financial difficulties, causing her home to go into foreclosure. Desperate, the lady decided to try God one more time. She got on her knees and prayed, saying, "I've already lost my husband, and I have no money to pay my bills. If You are real, please don't let me lose my home." Two nights before the scheduled foreclosure sale, she went to a local basketball tournament after her friends convinced her to get out of the house for an evening. At the game, a man approached her and asked if she remembered him. He said, "I'm the boy you bought the Eagle's basketball uniform for so I could play in the tournament. You and your husband would pick me up and take me to practice, too. Do you remember me?" "Why yes, you have grown up to be such a handsome young man. It's good to see you," the woman replied. *As she recognized the now adult man, he said, "I'm in the NBA now. I play for the Dallas Mavericks. I'm in town for a short break and I decided to come to the tournament to see if I could find your husband and thank him. If it wasn't for him, I never would have made it this far. Your husband was the first person who ever helped me to believe in myself. I must thank him. Where is he?" The man scanned the crowd to try to find the husband. The woman paused, and tears began to course down her cheeks. "What's the matter, ma'am," the man asked as he reached out to console her.*

"He's dead," the woman cried as he held her. She sat on the bleachers and told the NBA player the story, and he asked her if he could come by her home. As he entered the doors, he saw boxes stacked everywhere. He asked, "Why would you be moving at a time like this?" And she replied, "My house is being foreclosed on. It's not by my choice." She told the man about all her financial troubles and they both wept together. The NBA player decided to pay for the house in full, and he did so the next day through his accountant. He also paid off the woman's remaining bills. That marked the beginning of a new wonderful relationship. The woman and her husband had no children, and the NBA player, who grew up in a group home, had no parents. The woman became like a mother to the NBA player, and the NBA player took care of the woman as though she were his mother. They jointly created a foundation in the slain security officer's name, which actively fights crime, and the woman now runs the organization. The NBA player's kindness led the woman back to God. She knew after her experience that God cared for her greatly.

After the woman finished her story, she told Debbie, "Now I have to forgive you. I came to tell you that God loves you. Get your life together and serve Him. He will take your disaster and turn it into your testimony." *Debbie began to sob. She had no idea how her poor choices would lead to so much pain for so many others. She hugged the lady tightly and apologized. That day Debbie confessed her sins before God and turned her life over to Him. The woman and Debbie remain in touch, and the victim's wife even testified on Debbie's behalf at her sentencing.*

Now you have heard the stories of Maria, Keisha, and Debbie. What is your story? Who are your victims? What similarities does your story have with theirs, if any? Think about how drastically your crime could have affected so many others.

Who would know better than you and I how much pain we have caused our loved ones? Think about our children who have had to live without their mother. All the missed baseball games, movies, and graduations, because of our adverse actions. What about our parents, who count on us for love and support? What about their pain and their dark thoughts of having failed as parents? What about the other loved ones who supported us and are left behind, including spouses who are forced to shoulder all the bills? Think about what they must go through because of us.

When we consider the whole picture, we realize that our acts were selfish and unkind. In the end it was surely not worth it! We could have done the right thing, the correct way, and we would have been free of our pain and would have prevented injuries to others .

Now it's time to be a real woman and accept responsibility for our actions! For many of us, this will be the first time that we are truly remorseful for our crimes. It is not necessary to hold on to the guilt, but it is important to apologize to those we have hurt and ask God for forgiveness. We do this simply because it's what we should do. Are you ready to stand up and accept responsibility? If so, follow me in this prayer: *"God, today I realize the effects of my crime on others. Today I am truly remorseful. I admit I was wrong, and I ask that You please forgive me. Send Your divine healing to each one of my victims. Provide them with the love and support they need each day. Help them to also forgive me, and let them see how truly remorseful I am. I ask You today for another chance to make the correct decisions in life. Rekindle the bonds and ties of my family members and loved ones. Open their hearts to also forgive me. Today I stand before You as a new person. I promise to never make the same mistake of participating in any illegal activities. I now ask that You show me Your plan for my life, and lead and guide me in the way which I should go. Amen."*

Today, you took a huge step in your journey to restoration. You have released the negative mindsets that have held you captive. Now you can proceed forward and complete your mission. Congratulate yourself! You have demonstrated great maturity! Your actions have allowed the gates of freedom to open up. Soon you'll be walking through!

Chapter Questions

1) After reading the three examples in this chapter, do you view the effects of your crime differently? Why or why not?

2) What is the difference between acknowledging your shortcomings and your acceptance of responsibility?

3) Why is it necessary to accept responsibility for our adverse actions?

4) Now that you have viewed your crime from a victim's standpoint, would you be reluctant to commit the same crime again? Why or why not?

5) How do you feel now that you accepted responsibility for your actions?

WRITING ASSIGNMENT

Write a letter to one of the victims of your crime, which can include a family member or loved one. Ask them for forgiveness, and clearly state the actions you took that were wrong. Explain to them how you acknowledge their pain as a result of those actions, and outline for the victims what you are actively doing to permanently change your former ways.

CHAPTER 6

Closing the Doors to Shame and Guilt

I n the last two chapters, we've allowed ourselves to bring to the surface many hidden feelings of guilt, shame, and remorse. This was a necessary step to deal with our issues, so that we can successfully move ahead. We now need to be careful not to dwell on these negative emotions. In this chapter, we will acknowledge our feelings, and then release the ones that are creating havoc in our lives. We will accomplish this by learning to forgive ourselves.

We cannot change yesterday. What happened yesterday is done! It's our job to simply learn from our experiences, so that we will not continue to make the same mistakes. We've allowed ourselves to make the choice to expose our issues and weaknesses. This exposure has allowed us to clearly identify our shortcomings, so we can deal with them. We each have now been given an opportunity to improve our lives. Consider yourself blessed! Many people have died because of self-destruction. They never took the opportunity to change, so they died in the midst of their mess! Thank God that is not our fate! God has enlightened us with a road map to self improvement. Now it is up to us to discover its contents and follow the map!

In God's eyes, yesterday no longer counts. To Him, it's over and finished! Old things have passed away. Now He is ready for us to step into our new lives. God forgave us the moment we confessed our sins or our shortcomings to Him, now it is important that we forgive ourselves. We cannot stay trapped in guilt, shame, and remorse. These emotions will deplete us of our energies, and we will not be able to move forward in life. It is critical that we dust off the degradations of yesterday, and keep our eyes on the prize. LET THE PAST GO!!! It's over, it's finished, and it's done! The past has no bearing on your future; therefore, leave it all behind you!

God is so great and powerful! When we are ready for change, He can take everything that was meant for our harm and turn it around to work for our good. This is His nature and character. He's been so gracious to do it for so many others. He can do the same for you and for me! It is His will that we be happy and successful.

Before we were born, each of our lives was predestined. We were put on this Earth to complete an assignment, yet many of us have no clue what our worldly assignment is. Therefore we perceive our lives as being hopeless or unsuccessful. In this case God uses obstacles to enlighten us to see our purpose. Beat down and battered by life's obstacles, we falsely believe we are unloved by God, yet the truth is that the ones who experience the greatest hardships in life are usually God's chosen people. Yes, we are His favorites. This may be difficult to comprehend, but when God chooses leaders, it is so that the world will see His light shine through us. He uses our challenges to transform us into His own image. When people see us in our finished form, they will know without a doubt that God must have transformed us, and they will also be drawn to us because they desire the same results! All of the struggles we endured will help us to develop a deep concern and compassion for others who are experiencing similar setbacks to those we went through. We will then become instruments God can use to help save the lives of many others. That is the purpose in our pain and struggles. These adversities were sent to lead us to the light and to allow us to become a light to others who need us. If you've never experienced pain or struggle, you cannot experience growth. You would have no need to discover the truths about life, or to be led into your purpose. You also wouldn't be able to reach others who could truly profit from your help.

Think about it. I've watched church services in the prison chapel where a minister spoke about how he lived his life so perfectly and never made any mistakes, unlike the others around him. Before he could finish speaking, most of his audience of inmates had left the service. By the time he concluded, the chapel was almost empty. The problem was that the inmates could not identify with the speaker and all of his self-proclaimed goodness. On another occasion, I've been in a service where the visiting minister talked about how he had a rough life and did some terrible things that landed him in prison. In prison, he met God and turned his life around. He was originally sentenced to 30 years in prison, but he prayed to God and he stayed faithful to Him throughout his incarceration. The man told God that if He would give him another chance at life, this time he would serve God wholeheartedly and lead as many souls as he could to God. God answered this man's petition. Within the first seven years of his imprisonment, he met a lawyer who volunteered his services and helped the man overturn his conviction. The man was immediately released from prison, and ever since his release, he has been going into various prisons, preaching the Gospel to inmates. Guess what happened at that service? Almost every inmate in the building had tears streaming down their faces as the man told his story. He did an altar call and everyone got up and rededicated their lives to God.

I share this story because I want you to understand that once you turn your life around, your new life will speak to the multitudes! People will recognize the light inside you and admire your strength and your courage to have made the choice to change. This will encourage many others to want to change as well. Simply because of the light within you, you will be able to reach men and women whom no one else but you could have reached. It is your real-life experiences and hardships that allow people to identify with your story. They will realize that you have been through the same experiences as they have, so you will be "real" to them. People respond to "real" people. In days to come, when you change, instead of being looked down upon, you will be looked up to!

I want to assure you, God doesn't make mistakes! God knew you would meet those people and go down that road you took. He knew what that person was going to do to you, and He knew how it would affect your life. God allowed it to happen because He knew He would meet you right here, at the very point you are at today, called the "Point of Change." He also knew your struggle would make you strong. You've felt all this time that you were alone and living in turmoil, but what you did not know is that all along you've been in training. Your experience has made you an expert in overcoming. Now you will be able to deliver others from that same path of destruction you once walked along. When you are able to discover the purpose for your pain, it makes the pain bearable because you can see the meaning behind it. You can bear the storm when you are finally able to see the rainbow above you.

Keep on pursuing your purpose. Do not miss the mark! Your greatest breakthrough lies just ahead. In order to retrieve your prize, you must not look back! Yesterday is over; keep your eyes focused on today. Do what is right today and tomorrow will take care of itself. Tomorrow is going to be great! It's not going to be like anything you have ever witnessed before. So unload your heavy burdens of shame, fear, worry, doubt, guilt, and remorse. Move ahead and claim your prize! You are a mighty warrior! You overcame everything that life bitterly handed you; now you will overcome this hurdle too!

In this chapter we will learn how to break the bondage of shame and guilt. Before we can truly forgive ourselves, we must remove these negative emotions from our lives. They have kept many of us stagnant for a very long time, but today we will identify and uproot these long-lasting negative emotions that have plagued us.

In earlier chapters, we spoke about the enemy of our lives whom some refer to as Satan, who is sent to steal, kill and destroy us. He plots and schemes against us, using many of his devices and traps to keep us bound. Two weapons the enemy uses to paralyze us are thoughts of shame and thoughts of guilt that are injected into our minds. When we accept these thoughts as our own, they begin to overburden us, paralyze us, and deplete our energy.

Shame comes from the thought that we are bad people who are inadequate, and the belief that we create a problem by our mere existence. Shame is a sense of worthlessness that can turn into self pity, depression, and hopelessness. When life deals us many hard blows, we often begin to develop a sense of shame followed by the "Why me?" syndrome. These thoughts disable us and cause us to take our focus off the prize of success and acceptance of ourselves as we wallow in this negative emotion.

Guilt comes from something that we do. It is the remorse we feel when we know that we did something that was unethical or wrong. God uses this emotion to signal to us that we have moved off track. Once we detect the feeling of guilt, we must address our wrong actions, then immediately discard this emotion. The feeling of guilt has a positive purpose when it alerts us to the need to change our actions, but it can also be deadly if we hold on to it and do not dispose of it. Retained feelings of guilt can lead to serious depression, suicidal thoughts, and other self-destructive emotions. Always remember, none of us are perfect! We all make mistakes, so it's okay to feel guilty when we do something wrong. That is a signal to correct our behavior. When you feel guilty, fix the problem, change your behavior, and then move on. Do not stay stuck in guilt! If you do, the results will be fatal!

Many of us grew up feeling ashamed because of the false belief that our negative childhood experiences with abuse and neglect were our fault. We must break this thought pattern by understanding that any abuse or lack of love we suffered as children was not our fault. We are not responsible for the adverse actions of others. When we finally come into this revelation, we open the doors for healing to begin.

Shame makes a person feel worthless and like a burden to others. Shame causes us to feel that we are not worthy of the love, security, care, compassion, and attention of others. Shame causes us to establish the false belief that we aren't good people, that life is not worth living, and that we are something less than a beautiful, wonderful creation of God. Shame is very powerful! You cannot reach any level of success while you are mired in it. It creates deep-rooted confusion and serious distortions in our perception of "self." Instead of believing we made a mistake, we adopt the false belief that we are a mistake. Shame quickly blossoms into self-hate, which ultimately causes self-destruction.

The goal of the enemy is to make you quit. If you quit, you will not fulfill God's assignment for your life, and you will never help save the lives of the many who are assigned to benefit from your purpose. If you quit, the enemy wins! If he can convince you that you are worthless, stupid, dumb and inadequate, then he can stop you before you ever begin. Quitting means you will be unable to save the life of that young girl who has been assigned to you from God. You will not be in the right position to help your relatives who need your assistance. Quitting means that the youth center you were predestined to build, that would have created the positive childhood experiences of so many others, will never open. Quitting destroys the hope of your bright future and allows the enemy to win. It has been the enemy's goal all along to push you to give up. The enemy's actions are premeditated. He knows that if he stops you, he will also stop those who are counting on you. The feelings you have allowed to consume you are a trap set by the enemy. You must not believe his lies! Your life has purpose. It does have meaning! You are beautiful, made in God's own image. You can do anything that you set your mind to achieve. You will indeed be successful. All you have to do is make the choice to change. If you decide to change, change is indeed yours!

Guilt comes as result of our adverse actions. Our incarceration has caused many other hardships besides our own. When we are exposed to the pain we've inflicted on others, we become extremely remorseful, especially when we did not intend to cause anyone harm. Permanent feelings of remorse turn into guilt. Facing feelings of guilt in prison can be extremely difficult. We need to expose our feelings in order to deal with our issues. Now that we have acknowledged our problems, it is necessary that we let these negative emotions go! If we stay trapped in guilt, we will stay in a closed cycle of low self-esteem and destructive choices.

The guilty "self" unconsciously demands punishment or payback for the negative actions that we have taken. The guilty "self" imposes unhappiness, depression, a sense of unworthiness, and even physical damage. It causes chronic anger and resentment towards others, as we act out our inward feelings.

Unattended, guilt is a life sentence to self-destruction. The truth is that all of us have some measure of guilt that we harbor deep within, whether detected or not, relating to some matters of our past. We must address all our guilty feelings so we can release them and successfully heal.

Living in prison is a constant reminder of our negative actions. Each day, when we wake up in this environment, we are reminded of the events that led us here. Many of us are remorseful for our actions, yet we still have to face the punishment of imprisonment. We feel ashamed and guilty for what we have done, and we find it hard to forgive ourselves because we are still subject to the sentence that was imposed. We constantly replay our actions in our minds, repeating the "shoulda, coulda, woulda" syndrome, allowing ourselves to wallow in self-pity and depression. This cycle of negative thoughts prevents us from moving forward.

Once you have experienced remorse and have acknowledged the wrongdoings that led you to imprisonment, you must let it go! Take the next step, which is to look for the good that can come from this bad situation. Discover how you can use this time to help develop "self." Stop considering prison as simply a punishment. Look at it as a gift. The gift is the free time we need to examine our patterns and old behaviors so that we can change them. We have been granted another chance at life! The woman who died last night from an overdose will not be granted another chance to make a change. View this sentence as a blessing instead of a burden. When you are released from prison you will be ahead of the game. Many others you left behind will be in the same place years from now. They have not yet chosen to put in the work required to become successful. You will get out of prison and soar, surpassing the many who haven't taken this journey! You don't know yet all the wonderful plans God has in store for you! Maybe He wants to rekindle the broken ties within your family, to enable you to continue your education so that you can get that great job He has for you. Or maybe He will lead you to detach from the destructive relationships you just couldn't break free from. Whatever your circumstance is, God has a plan, and His plans are always good! There is a purpose and a reason for everything, even your incarceration.

Spending time in prison, I've witnessed so many miracles. I've seen addicts quit their habits and turn their lives around. I've seen husbands and wives reunite. I've seen women prepare for promising careers, and, most frequently, I've witnessed many early releases. When the "cake is baked," or the purpose of our imprisonment is met, we are released and free to go! Many of us are prolonging our stay because of our resistance to open up our consciousness to become aware of the areas we need to improve. Therefore, we resist change. It is important that we surrender, let go, and let God have His way in our lives.

It is vital that you take this opportunity to forgive yourself. Constantly reliving your past and feeling sorry for yourself will not benefit your future. You must release these negative emotions, and never look back.

Self-forgiveness can heal us from all our toxic shame and guilt. It is the act of learning from our past while being reminded of our inherent goodness in the present. Self-forgiveness is at the heart of our healing process. Self-forgiveness is the only instrument we can use that insures we will move ahead and not repeat the same old mistakes. It essentially gives us will power. Self-forgiveness creates and restores our self-worth and self-esteem. You cannot move forward without self-forgiveness.

In Robin Casarjian's book, *Houses of Healing*, she cleverly illustrates the true meaning of self-forgiveness and the steps to obtain self-forgiveness. True self-forgiveness takes time, courage, and honesty. Few people have a real understanding of what it means to forgive themselves, because they lack guidance and support. We are blessed to have a clear road map that defines this true self-forgiveness.

Self-forgiveness is not redefining an offense as non-offensive. We cannot downplay our past actions. We must evaluate honestly what occurred and reposition ourselves not to take the same course of action again.

Self-forgiveness does not condone behavior that is hurtful, insensitive, and abusive, or that lacks integrity. It is acknowledging our past negative behavior patterns and adopting new healthy behavioral habits.

Self-forgiveness does not excuse or overlook our flaws nor does it diminish the importance or the impact of our actions. Self-forgiveness allows us to completely explore our actions, expose our wounds, and position ourselves to heal, releasing us from the past. Self-forgiveness should never be equated with avoidance of responsibility or remorse for our past. We need to be remorseful in the process of self-forgiveness. That remorse is the energy we use to ignite permanent change.

The key action necessary to complete the process of self-forgiveness is our alignment with "self." As we align with "self" we awaken to wisdom and compassion, which are the ingredients necessary to make better conscious choices. Better choices enable us to increase self-respect and give us a healthy sense of responsibility towards ourselves and others. Better choices also increase our courage and belief in "self," which is needed to pursue our dreams and goals.

When we become in tune with our true "self," we naturally begin to experience greater peace and faith, which supplies us with strength. We begin to offer ourselves gentleness, love, and compassion that will allow us to appreciate our experiences and grow from them. It is our alignment with "self" or the consciousness of our inherent goodness that helps us forgive ourselves.

The purpose of self-forgiveness is to shine light on our fears and destructive judgments that have kept us bound. In many cases, we have been our own jailer, holding ourselves in a self-imposed prison. Self-forgiveness is the challenge of being accountable and learning to know, accept, and love ourselves, despite our past experiences in life. Self-forgiveness is the mark of a new day that separates our past and propels us into the future.

"Your situation is just transportation to your destination," Pastor Joel Osteen has been quoted as saying. Accept life as it has happened. The events of our past were necessary. They are now the bridges we will use to cross to our future. "Losers focus on what they're going through. Winners focus on where they're going to," Pastor Joel Osteen also states. Take hold of these words and turn your eyes on your future.

Are you ready to focus on what awaits you? Are you finally ready to leave your past behind and forgive yourself? Will you join me in this pursuit of freedom? If so, let's say this affirmation together: *"God created me in His own image, therefore I am beautiful. Greatness lies within me but it is up to me to tap into this power. Today I am ridding myself of all the shame and guilt that has tortured me. I have acknowledged and accepted responsibility for my adverse behavior patterns, and I will no longer operate in them. They will no longer hold me back from my bright future. Today I am a brand new creature. Old things are now passed away. I will only focus on those things that will help me in my journey going forward. Today I honestly forgive myself. Self, I love you, and I will do everything in my power to protect you. I will care for you and not put you in situations that can risk your harm or place you in danger ever again. Today marks a new day! Today I am free from my past to move ahead!"*

Congratulations! You have taken a big step! You have done what many others could not do. You have finally unloosened the shackles that have been weighing you down. You are now able to move ahead in excellence.

Guilt and shame may try to sneak back in, but don't let them! You have already dealt with the past. Refuse to relive it. It's difficult to maintain our freedom from guilt and shame when others constantly bring our past to our attention. When this happens, do not deny the past or even make excuses. Simply tell the person, "Oh, you are talking about the old me. Baby, she's buried and gone. I don't want to talk about her, let's talk about the new me. She's fabulous and she's doing great things! Would you like to hear about her plans?" Refuse to dwell on the past, and you'll stay energized to move ahead.

Let's close this chapter with a short prayer: *"God, I thank You for exposing my feelings of guilt and shame. I have dealt with them and today I released them. I did what at times seemed impossible to do: I forgave myself. Therefore, I am no longer bound by my past. Today I ask that You give me the strength to keep all guilt and shame from creeping back into my life. I ask that You lead positive people into my life, and rid me of those who would try to hinder me or constantly have me relive my past. Please give me the strength I need to sustain my freedom. Amen."*

CHAPTER QUESTIONS
1) What is guilt?
2) What is shame?
3) Why are guilt and shame toxic to our emotional health?
4) How do we rid ourselves of guilt and shame?
5) What is self-forgiveness?

WRITING ASSIGNMENT

Write down the events that have caused you the most shame and guilt. Then list what you can do to fix each situation. If you cannot remedy the problem, write: "There is nothing I can do to fix this situation." Describe what you will do to ensure a better future, and how you will not repeat the same mistakes. These actions will be a part of your written plans for a greater future.

CHAPTER 7

Forgiving Others Who Have Wronged Us

I n the last chapter, we learned how to eliminate our shame and guilt by forgiving ourselves. For many of us, this was a difficult but much needed healing process, because shame and guilt had paralyzed our lives. In addition to forgiving ourselves, we must rid ourselves of the bondage that has been holding us back from moving forward victoriously. In this chapter, we will learn about the importance of forgiving all the people in our lives who have hurt us. Once again, this may not be an easy process. In most instances forgiving will require strength and courage, but it is a vital prerequisite to freeing ourselves from the burdens of our past.

The root of most offender behavior is a result of unhealed anger, rage, grief, guilt, and shame from childhood issues. Many of us were abused as children. Whether it was actual physical abuse or emotional abuse, many of us have suffered from traumatic events as a child that have influenced us to become what we were.

Many of us remember the abuse that was inflicted upon us as children very vividly. The experiences are often too painful to fully recount. Therefore, we bury these experiences, yet we hold on to the resentment towards our abusers. We know it was their malicious actions that caused us to develop the many behavioral problems with which we have struggled. As victims of childhood abuse, we feel weak and vulnerable, causing many of us to counteract these feelings by also becoming an abuser. We have felt as though we needed to be courageous and strong on the outside so that no one would ever be able to abuse us again. We took matters into our own hands, and we built walls of protection around ourselves. Putting up these self-made walls blocked us from exchanging love with others. Inevitably we became a part of the destructive cycle that engulfed us. That cycle will exist until we rise up and break it! The only way to break the cycle of hate is by creating a new cycle of love. Love has the power to heal, set free, and deliver. As we begin to allow love to embrace us, it will break the cycle of hate, not only within us, but also within the ones who inflicted pain on us.

The cycle of love begins with forgiveness. Just as God has forgiven us, we must forgive those who trespassed against us. Some of us may not have suffered abuse as children. Others may have been abused, betrayed, raped, or even mistreated as teens or adults. Regardless of our treatment we still carry the baggage of being a victim. Therefore, it's important that we honestly examine these emotions and overcome them, so that we no longer remain the victim. Instead we can become the victor!

You must remember that it was the enemy's plan to prepare terrible situations and circumstances as traps to keep us in bondage. He knows the great plans God has for each of us, and his job is to try to stop them. Unforgiveness is one of our enemy's biggest traps. He knows God will not forgive us until we forgive others. Many of us have been praying to God for a long time and are not receiving answers to our prayers because of our unforgiveness. It is God's law that we forgive! We cannot get around it. If we refuse to obey His commands, we are blocked from receiving His blessings. We cannot be victorious in life with hatred, bitterness, and unforgiveness in our hearts. We remove these negative emotions by allowing ourselves to forgive, realizing that forgiveness is for us. It is not for our abusers. As long as we remain frozen in resentment and bitterness, we will not move forward. Therefore, we must do ourselves a favor and forgive all those who have harmed us!

One of the greatest mistakes we can make in life is to try to avenge ourselves, or try to get even with others who have harmed or offended us. This only creates further havoc and bitterness within us. We must trust the fact that God sees and knows all things. If we pray and put our problems in God's hands, He will vindicate us every time! When we stop being angry about all that has happened to us, and we stop seeking revenge on those who have harmed us, God's justice will balance out the tables! He will take what was meant to harm us and make it work in our favor. He has the power to make our enemies our footstool. In the end, He will promote us because of our faithfulness and obedience. Therefore, the best revenge is success! God is the only one that can bring about real justice, and He will do it in ways we never imagined possible. Stop taking matters into your own hands! If you want to see real results, turn your problems over to God.

One of my favorite ministers on television is Dr. Joyce Meyer. She has a huge ministry and is an author of several dozen books. She is also a large supporter of prison ministry. Many of you may have seen her books on the shelves in prison. This woman has an awesome testimony. She grew up in a small town, Fenton, Missouri. She had a father who sexually molested her for many years when she was a child. Her mother was aware of her father's actions, yet her mother was too intimidated to stop it. Joyce grew up feeling lonely, confused, bitter and betrayed. At a young age, she married an abusive man, and the couple had a little boy. Life was very rough for her. She became bitter and angry as a result. Joyce was living in a poor neighborhood in a trailer home. She decided one day to split from her husband, and she was introduced to God. Her life was in shambles, and she felt hopeless. Shortly after that, she met a man who took great interest in her, and he eventually asked her to marry him. He was a good, hard-working Christian man, Dave Meyer, and he is now her husband. Together they grew as Christians. They went through many growth struggles during the earlier years of their marriage, but they helped to balance each other and became supportive partners in their relationship.

Today Dr. Joyce Meyer has one of the biggest ministries in the world. She preaches the Word of God to the multitudes. She reaches out to an audience of women who were also once abused. Her father is now deceased, but before he died she made amends with him and her mother, and they both apologized to Joyce. In the end, her father became very sick, and Joyce and her husband purchased a home for him and her mother, and they cared for both parents. Joyce's love and forgiveness towards her father convinced him to turn his life over to God, and he did so before he died.

Joyce preaches her message of love throughout the world and has saved millions of lives. Today she is very wealthy, and is a renowned author who sells millions of copies of her books. The woman who was once poor, broken, and hopeless is now achieving great success that many others only dream of achieving. She is no longer ashamed of her abuse – it is now her testimony. Her testimony is "real" and it touches the hearts of her audience. How many lives will be touched and saved by your story? The success that has happened for Joyce can also happen to you. It all starts with forgiveness. Are you willing to forgive?

We can learn to develop mercy when we look at the actions of our abusers. Mercy is the ability to see beyond what was done to us and discover the reason why it happened. To many of us, this may sound ludicrous. We think to ourselves, "Well, they abused me, and it is not my job to care why they did it." We haven't yet understood the fact that when we discover the "why," it helps us develop compassion for the offender. It also reminds us who our real enemy is- Satan, not our actual abuser. Many times people have acted out and they don't even understand the reason for what they did. Negative thoughts were sent to them by our true enemy, and they chose to act on them, not realizing it was a set-up. Think about how many times serial killers and others who do malicious acts claim they heard a voice that told them to do it. We may view them as being crazy, but in fact that is how the enemy works! He puts thoughts into people's minds. Some are strong enough to cast away these thoughts, others are not that strong, and so they fall into the trap. Usually, these are people who were also victimized, so they think that what they are doing is acceptable. Their minds become numb to their actions, allowing them to do the unthinkable. They live out the ideas that overtook their minds. That is why it is important that we learn to control and monitor our thoughts. We aren't the only "victims," our abusers are also victims. They have been used by the enemy to victimize us. Blinded by deception, they fell into his evil scheme. Instead of hating these people, we need to pray that God will enlighten them to acknowledge their wrongdoings and to change their lives. When we are able to pray for our abusers, we are ready to embrace true forgiveness.

Unforgiveness is deadly, and produces a root of bitterness that poisons our entire system. Many people have died of diseases that stemmed from the negative energy of unforgiveness. Resentment and bitterness are a form of bondage that holds us captive. That is why it is important that, when people offend us, we don't replay the offense repeatedly in our minds. When we do that, we develop a deep-rooted bitterness which can turn into hate. These feelings of hate, when allowed to set in, are hard to dispel. The only way to recover from a hurtful offense is to pray about it. Turn the problem over to God, then stop thinking and talking about the issue. When it arises in your thoughts, cast it out of your mind. If you can't do that, go back to God with your concerns in prayer. Ask Him to remove the resentment, hurt, and bitterness, and He will heal you!

Many of us are unable to go to God for help because we hold unforgiveness towards Him. We spoke about this matter in Chapter 2. Some of us blame God for cheating us out of what we felt was important to us. We feel as though God had the power to change these events if He wanted to, but He did not, so we blame Him. We feel neglected and let down by God, so we abandoned Him, removing Him from our lives. This is not a solution and can be very detrimental to our well-being. We all need God! God is good, even when we can't understand why He does what He does. He is perfect, and His thoughts far exceed our ability to comprehend them. Anything that happens in our lives, God has allowed it to occur, because He has a plan to make something good out of it. We must trust that He has chosen the best outcome for us. This is hard for many of us to comprehend, because we are stuck in the "right now" of our situations. In our current conditions, we are looking for immediate results and immediate gratification. God does not work like that! Life is His obstacle course. We must experience the many ups and downs that lead us to growth and purpose. Obstacles are God's tools to build us up and strengthen us.

It is our job to look for the good in every situation and not focus on the negative. Your life happened as it did to place you on the path to freedom. Your journey came with many obstacles, but now you are strong! The small things you will now experience in life will be like dusting the dirt off your shoulders. Why? Life has taught you what to value. You have learned from your lessons. Subsequently, you will now travel much more smoothly along the pathways of life. Your life now has purpose and meaning! Recognize the good and discard the rest. Most importantly, do not blame God. Praise God! He is good!

Unforgiveness becomes self-imprisonment. To be held by old grievances prevents us from moving ahead. Not to forgive is to yield our lives to the control of another. It handcuffs us to the person we resent, and it keeps us emotionally bound to our abusers.

People often think that if we forgive someone, we are doing that person an undeserved favor by letting them off the hook. They don't understand that in actuality we are doing ourselves a bigger favor by forgiving the other person. Through forgiveness, we break emotional attachments to our abusers. Anger and resentment require our energy to keep these emotions alive. We become emotionally bound to the person we resent by constantly giving them our attention, which then fuels these negative emotions. Forgiveness is an act of self-interest. It allows us to break free from these destructive thoughts that have the potential to weaken our bodies and minds and ultimately kill us. We forgive so we won't allow our emotions to be driven by someone else's ignorance, fears, and problems. When we forgive, we restore the personal power that we had lost through unforgiveness.

Forgiveness is not pretending or ignoring our true feelings. It is not acting as if everything is fine. Forgiveness doesn't mean you approve of or support the behavior of the person that caused you pain. It also doesn't mean that you should hesitate to take the actions needed to change your situation. You do not have to associate with or befriend your abuser! Forgiveness means you simply detach from all hateful and angry feelings towards this person.

Forgiveness is the inner emotion of letting go of the offense that was perpetrated against you. Forgiveness is acknowledging that person's ignorance, removing yourself from the situation as quickly as possible, and then releasing the negative emotions they have caused you to feel. Forgiveness does not mean you have to tell the person who offended you, "I forgive you," unless that is what you choose. Forgiveness is not about them, it is about you! If you can vocalize your forgiveness, that is great and probably a sign that you have truly forgiven that person, but the choice is up to you. As long as you successfully detach from all feelings of hatred, bitterness, and resentment, you have fulfilled your obligation to forgive.

Forgiveness is not forgetting the act; it is releasing the negative emotions that keep you bound by the act. When you truly forgive a person who has hurt you, you can remember what they have done, but you are no longer bound to the "sting" of what took place. It's like a bee that is still buzzing around, but whose stinger has been removed. Forgiveness is not just an action; it is a new perception of your abuser and a new perspective of the circumstances that influenced your abuser. Forgiveness teaches us that, under behavior that appears heartless, there is a heart. Regardless of what our abusers have done to us, they are still souls that have value to God. Hate only fuels their behavior; these people need love. We show them our love by forgiving them and praying for them. Remember, we are not to forgive the act; we are to forgive the person. We forgive their ignorance, their suffering, and their confusion. When we change our perception, we change our emotional reactions. Forgiveness says we can disagree with someone and their actions without having to keep our hearts closed by remaining angry.

Forgiveness in many cases is not easy because of the pain it may cause. Regardless of our suffering, we must forgive. Caring for "self" starts with learning to forgive. Don't remain handcuffed to your abusers a day longer than necessary. You possess the keys to your freedom! The power is in your hands. Unlock the doors to bondage and forgive!

If you have chosen to move forward in life and forgive all those who have hurt you or caused you harm, follow me in this prayer: *"God, You know all that I have experienced. You know every offense and abuse that has been committed against me. I ask that You give me the strength to forgive all those who have trespassed against me. I turn all of these abusive events and my abusers over to You now. I ask that You heal me of all the defilement that has been left in my life because of these offenses. Please deliver me from the hurt and pain I feel because of these events. I pray that You open the eyes of all those who have abused, mistreated, and betrayed me. Allow them to recognize that they have been used by the enemy. Touch their hearts and lead them onto the road of restoration. Help me to change my perception of the events and circumstances that have hindered me from achieving Your purpose for my life. Help me to recognize the good You have intended to come out of every obstacle, even in the midst of my turmoil. Please forgive me for any feelings of anger, resentment, bitterness, and unforgiveness towards You and anyone else for whom I may have harbored these feelings. I now understand You have a plan and a reason greater than I could ever imagine. I know the plans You have for me lead to the road of restoration. Please lead and guide me into this plan. Keep me covered and protected from the schemes of the enemy. Shower me with Your love, affection, and favor all the days of my life. Most importantly, give me a heart that always forgives. Amen."*

You are almost finished with this chapter. There is one last thing you must do. Stop and recall to your mind all those who have deeply hurt, betrayed, or abused you. Write down their names, and the key part of what they did to hurt you, in the Abuser's Chart located in Chapter 7 of your *Voices of Consequences, "Unlocking the Prison Doors"* Workbook/ Journal. Also complete the activities in that section of the journal. When you are finished, complete this affirmation:

"Today, (list the names of your abusers), I am no longer emotionally bound to you. What you have done to me will no longer affect me. I realize today you are also a victim that has been used by the enemy. I have decided that I will no longer allow myself to have feelings of bitterness, anger, hate or resentment towards you. I exercise my right to love you. I will love you by praying that God will open your eyes and allow you to see the pain you have caused me and others. My prayer is that you will one day change. In the meantime, I detach myself from you emotionally by forgiving you. Today I am free!"

Wow! That was very brave. You did it! You have now officially completed this step. It took a great deal of willingness and courage to get here. You have now dumped everyone's trash out of your can! You can live today confident that yesterday is no longer attached to you. Move ahead! Don't look back. Your journey called "freedom" has officially begun.

CHAPTER QUESTIONS
1) What is forgiveness?
2) What is unforgiveness?
3) Why are people so reluctant to forgive others?
4) Why is unforgiveness dangerous?
5) What misconceptions do people have of what must be done in order to forgive?

94

WRITING ASSIGNMENT

> Write a letter to the person(s) who harmed you the most. Tell them how their actions have affected you and how they made you feel. Recount the moment by expressing it on paper. Release all your feelings. Then close the letter by informing the person(s) that you forgive them. From the teachings, detail the ways in which they are also a victim of the enemy. Convince your abuser(s) to open their eyes, and encourage them to change their ways.

(Note: You do not have to give this letter to the person(s) unless you so choose. This letter is to help you let go of what's trapped inside. Let this be the last and final time you take yourself through this emotional process. Write it all down, and then release your feelings by forgiving your abuser(s).)

CHAPTER 8

Changing Our "Stinking Thinking"

Throughout this series, we've been learning how to change our views and perspectives concerning life's issues. This requires constant work, which is necessary to improve our lives. Many of us have landed in various adverse positions based on our impaired thinking. Our beliefs allowed us to make misjudgments. In order to change our lives we must first change our thinking. In this chapter, we will learn the importance of positive thinking. We will also discover how to uproot our "stinking thinking," and how to replace negative thoughts with positive thoughts.

The issue of our thinking is crucial to our current experiences. Our thoughts are what forge our actions. Everything we do first starts with a thought. As thoughts develop we act on them, and they become our actions. Nothing occurs without thought. We develop our behavior patterns and our plans for life based on what we think. In order to do something, rightly or wrongly, we must first think about it. As we hold on to our thoughts, they eventually become our experiences.

Whatever we set in our minds will eventually be what we hold in our hands! When we learn to change our thought patterns to produce good, healthy thoughts, and make those dominant, we will begin to experience and feel the fruits of that process in our lives. We hold the power, which lies in the choices we make in our thinking. As we rearrange our thoughts, we will automatically rearrange our lives! The root of our problems stem from the wrong thinking patterns we have assimilated from others. In order to overcome, we have to break those adverse thinking habits.

To truly understand the importance of thoughts, we must explore the law of attraction. The law of attraction is a universal law that states "like attracts like," which means as you think a thought, you are also attracting like thoughts to you. Therefore, whatever thoughts we have been consumed with have resulted in our current experiences. If you have been experiencing angry thoughts, your life is now full of anger and chaos. If you have been experiencing happy, pleasant thoughts, your life is now full of good, healthy, peaceful experiences. We all are a result of our past thinking. What kind of life are you experiencing now? It is the result of the thoughts you have been sending out into the atmosphere. If we want to experience a good life, we must fill your minds with positive thoughts. Those positive thoughts will send a signal to the universe to return to us more of what we are thinking. Our minds become like boomerangs, bringing back what we send out. Therefore, our good thoughts will ultimately bring us good experiences.

The law of attraction may be new to some of us, but it is true! This law is just as real and relevant as the law of gravity, which is the reason we are able to stand up straight without falling down. The law of attraction governs our experiences. I recommend that you read Rhonda Byrnes' best seller, *The Secret*. This book details the law of attraction. This spiritual law has been the "secret" of wealthy, successful people for many centuries. They have learned to change their lives and their experiences based on changing their thinking. We are no different from these people. We can achieve the same success by conquering our "stinking thinking."

According to the law of attraction, the only reason why people do not have what they want is because they are thinking incorrectly. In this case, their thoughts are focused more on what they don't want rather than what they do want. We cannot passively allow depressing thoughts of defeat to flood our minds. When we do, negative situations arise as a result. We attract to us the things we think about. This is why it is important, regardless of what we are going through, that we stop and make an active decision to control our thinking. Negative thoughts create anxiety, worry, doubt, and fear. The more we think this way, the more it will become our reality. The only solution is to release these negative thoughts as quickly as we detect them. Our feelings are our indicators that let us know the types of thoughts we are having. When we are feeling bad, that is our indicator that we need to change our thoughts. Regardless of our circumstances, it is important that we recognize the good that can come from our situation. When we learn to search out the good, we begin to experience good positive thoughts. Those thoughts radiate into the atmosphere and bring about positive results in our lives. As we change our perception, which is ultimately changing our thoughts, we also change our experience. Instantly our bad situations become bearable, because we are able to recognize the light that shines at the end of the tunnel. This positive energy brings about positive events into our lives. The correct perspective is essentially our "miracle" in life. It is our shift in cognitive thought that molds our vision and sculpts our realities.

Think about mornings when you woke up late, tripped over a shoe, and fell, or maybe you received bad news. After these events, the whole day seemed to be thrown off course. Why? Unconsciously or consciously, you said in your mind today is going to be a bad day and you ended up getting just what you thought. We negate such situations by declaring in our minds that we will only experience good, positive results each day. When we make a conscious effort to experience the good, we will get just that because we will expect it. Whatever you look for in life will become your experience. Many of us have been unconsciously expecting failure, mishaps, or hard times. We are now experiencing the results of our "stinking thinking." The good news is we don't have to stay in that pit! We can overcome by changing our thoughts, and controlling our thinking. We control our thoughts by choosing what we will or will not allow ourselves to consider. It must become our goal to purposely infuse our minds with good thoughts!

The Bible also confirms the importance of our thought life. In Proverbs, Chapter 23, verse 7 it states: "As a man thinketh in his heart, so is he." This verse instructs that man is literally what he thinks. Our character is the complete sum of all our thoughts. Noble character is not by chance. It is by a concentrated effort of right thinking. Therefore, we have the power to change our character!

In the 1800s, James Allen wrote a book entitled *As a Man Thinketh*. This book is excellent. Mr. Allen compares man's mind to a garden, which may be intelligently cultivated or allowed to run wild; whether cultivated or neglected, the mind must, and will, bring forth its fruit. If no useful seeds are placed in our minds, then we will produce an abundance of useless weeds. These useless weeds are our "stinking thinking." Just as a gardener cultivates his plot, keeping it free from weeds and growing flowers and fruits, so must we tend to the garden of our minds, as is Mr. Allen's advice. In order to be prosperous, we must weed out all wrong, useless, and impure thoughts, and clear our minds of our "stinking thinking." Then we must replace these thoughts with pure, positive, healthy thoughts!

Mr. Allen also states, "Every man is where he is by the law of his being, the thoughts which he has built into his character have brought him there, and in the arrangement of his life there is no element of chance, but all is the result of a law which cannot err." He also states, "A man does not come to the almshouse or the jail by the tyranny of fate or circumstance, but by the pathway of groveling thoughts and base desires." If we accept these statements as fact, our current circumstances are all a result of our thought life. Allen further states, "If a man radically alters his thoughts he will be astonished at the rapid transformation it will effect in the material conditions of his life." This statement provides the key to our freedom. As we change our thoughts, we rapidly transform our life. The key to unlocking the prison doors is in our minds.

The Bible gives us further instructions on how to transform our minds. Philippians, Chapter 4, verse 8 states, "Whatever things are noble, whatever things are just, whatever things are pure, whatever things are lovely, whatever things are of good report, if there is any virtue and if there is anything praiseworthy - mediate on these things." There is a reason for this instruction. Whatever we meditate on or think about, will become our experience. Our thoughts affect our attitudes and our moods. If you do not like the way you are feeling, that indicates you need to change your thoughts. When you begin to start feeling good that indicates you are on the right track. It is positive thoughts that lay the groundwork for a prosperous future.

The way to experience a good life is to hold onto the good moments. When we feel good, we must purposely hold onto these feelings and let nothing snatch them away from us. As we maintain these feelings, we open the door to a continuous flood of like experiences. It feels great to feel good!

Life's purpose is enjoyment. We will encounter obstacles and adverse circumstances, but it is up to us to enjoy our journey. Obstacles create opportunities to expand our knowledge. As we expand our wisdom and knowledge, we are promoted. Promotion includes financial gain and emotional maturity.

Now that we understand the importance of our thoughts, let's take a more in-depth look into our behavioral patterns and past thoughts that have affected our lives.

As we have learned, our minds are the forerunners of our actions, and our actions are a direct result of our thinking. It is our negative mindsets that have created our adverse circumstances. The root of all our problems has been our "stinking thinking." The only solution is to learn how to renew our minds with correct thinking.

In previous chapters, we discussed that we all have an enemy whose job it is to destroy our lives. This enemy was assigned prior to our existence. From the moment we were born, he has been patiently plotting against us. This same enemy offers us wrong thinking patterns. Our job is to recognize the thoughts he offers us and not accept them. When we receive such thoughts in our minds, we must immediately kick them out. Do not accept the bait! When we accept wrong thoughts, we develop "strongholds" in our minds. Strongholds are negative beliefs that are contrary to correct and noble thinking. Strongholds make us believe we are right, when in actuality we are wrong. Strongholds disable our consciousness, making us feel as if it is okay to practice acts that are wrong. These bad acts ultimately lead us into self-destruction, and they stop us from receiving the good God has intended for us.

Strongholds are also created to decrease our faith in ourselves. They are the whispered lies in our minds that tell us, "You aren't good enough," "Things will never work out," and "You are destined to fail." When we begin to think these statements and accept them as our own, we accept the package. Remember the law of attraction. Our thoughts become our experiences. Our enemy knows that whatever we think and believe we will ultimately receive. Therefore, he uses discouragement as a trap. Have you been tricked into taking his bait?

Our circumstances do not dictate our destiny. It is the way that we perceive our circumstances that determine the results we will get. Let's explore an example of two sisters who grew up in the same household, yet experienced two separate outcomes in life.

EXAMPLE:

Two sisters, Denise and Ladonna, grew up in the inner city of Chicago, Illinois, in a single-parent home. Life was difficult for both girls as children and adolescents. Their mother worked two jobs to make ends meet. She was hardly ever home to care for the girls, so they practically raised themselves. Denise resented the fact that her mother was seldomly there for her. As a result, she became very rebellious. Ladonna realized her mother was only doing what she needed to do to provide for her family, so she accepted her mother's absence. As soon as Ladonna turned 16, she got a part-time job to assist her mother with the bills.

Denise grew up disliking school. Although she was the older sister, she required help from Ladonna with her studies. Throughout her life she viewed schoolwork as difficult. She always said in her mind, "I can't do this! This is too much for me!" Eventually she ended up quitting school. She dropped out in the 9th grade. Ladonna, on the other hand, preserved even though she found it challenging at first to grasp the work. Unlike her peers, she had no one to help her with homework. Instead of giving up, Ladonna relied on her teachers for extra assistance. Her determination paid off. She maintained an A+ average and graduated high school at the top of her class.

Meanwhile, Denise's life quickly began to spiral downhill. Her resentment and rebellion at home led her to join a local gang. She rapidly began to pick up the behavioral patterns and beliefs of the gang members. She saw gang life as "fun." She felt as though her new sisters and brothers in the gang loved her and that they "had her back." Denise quit school and moved out of her mother's house. She moved in with one of the leaders of the gang who became the father of her two children. Denise grew accustomed to the gang life, and she enjoyed the esteem and respect she received from her peers. Denise saw the money rolling in. She felt as though this was the only way to live life! She thought, "I'll never have to work hard like my mother. I'll be there for my kids, and I'll have lots of money."

For several years Denise raised her kids and gave them everything she didn't have growing up. This satisfaction made her arrogant. Although she was promoted to second-in-command in the gang, under her children's father, Denise was the true boss. She was all about her money! She did whatever it took to keep the money flowing in, including injuring other parties, if need be. She had a no-nonsense attitude, and she meant business! Denise took no shorts. It was her dedication and determination that helped grow the gang's empire. Eventually Denise and her children's father ran three separate neighborhoods. Their fame and "hood" notoriety quickly spread, causing them to get under the skin of local rivals. They even gained the attention of the FBI. Other rivals tried to creep into her place. As a result, there were blood baths throughout the inner cities of Chicago. The heat was on. The FBI was on Denise and so were her rivals!

One day Denise arrived at her children's school to discover someone had picked them up from school, which she hadn't authorized Denise was frantic. Her children meant everything to her. This event dramatically affected her. Denise reached out to her mother and her sister Ladonna, who was now a respected lead detective in a Chicago suburb. The girls hadn't connected in years, because the two had separate interests. Ladonna heard about Denise's children's plight, and her heart ached with compassion. Ladonna called up one of her friends, a special agent in the FBI. Reluctant to get involved after he realized who Denise and her kids' father were, the agent finally agreed to help when he saw the deep concern of Ladonna. The agent arranged a stakeout by convincing Denise and her children's father to give up their lifestyle and assist the FBI in helping track down their rivals. The children were recovered after the FBI raided the ransom meeting location. Denise got back her children, but she and her husband were immediately charged with racketeering.

Ladonna took care of Denise's children while Denise awaited sentencing. Denise was looking at a life sentence, but by the grace of God, the agent showed her favor and testified about the assistance he had obtained from her. Denise ended up with a 10-year sentence, of which she would have to complete 7 years. Denise thought prison was the end of the road for her. At first she didn't think she would make it. She was sent to Danbury Federal Correctional Institution in Danbury, Connecticut, which was far away from her home. While imprisoned, she earned her GED and enrolled in the culinary arts program, where she received her chef's certification. Relations between Denise and her family became very tight. Denise begin to talk to her mother, and she finally understood why her mother had to work so hard to take care of her family. Denise's mother and LaDonna took care of

Denise and her children while she was in prison. The entire family became very close.

Denise was released from prison a year early after completing the Bureau of Prisons' R.D.A.P. drug program. Denise landed a job as an assistant chief at a local restaurant and did very well. She had great leadership skills, and everyone loved her. The owner decided to sell the business, and Denise thought she would be out of a job. Denise told her mother and sister about her troubles. Her mom came to the job and spoke with the owner. Her mother had been saving her money for many years. Denise's mother decided to buy the restaurant. The restaurant is now a family-run business that is very successful. Denise's kids even work part-time at the restaurant. Today the family is enjoying a joyous, prosperous life!

Let's analyze this story: Denise and Ladonna grew up in the same house under the same conditions, yet one daughter became a leader of a gang and the other became a lead detective. What was the difference between the girls? The difference was their thinking. Denise refused to understand why her mother couldn't spend extra time with her. In her mind, she believed her mother didn't love her. These negative thoughts led her to rebel against her mother. Ladonna had a correct perspective of why her mother was unable to spend quality time with her children; her correct thinking led her to work hard and try to change her current experiences. It was Denise's wrong thoughts that led her in the wrong direction in life. Her thoughts attracted the gang members who filled her with more negative thought patterns. Everything remained chaotic, until she found herself in prison. There, she changed her thought patterns. She no longer wanted to live her old lifestyle, so she looked for a way to change. She studied for her GED and culinary arts certification. As a result, she began to erase and defeat old negative thinking habits by creating new positive thoughts. Her new attitude led her to a better life.

Where did you go wrong in your thinking? Who helped influence your bad thoughts? When did you decide to change your thinking? How has your life been as a result? These are questions you need to ask yourself.

We can change our thoughts by surrounding ourselves with positive people who are productive members of society. Just as we followed negative people, we can persistently follow positive people and become successful.

Prison allows us time to improve our thinking, and we can do this by reading positive books about how to improve ourselves and about others who overcame their obstacles. Reading uplifting books helps us to change our thinking habits. Continue along in the *Voices of Consequences Enrichment Series*. This series includes five additional books along with a daily meditation book that teaches imprisoned women how to improve their lives and how to successfully transition back into the free world. Positive books like these will keep your mind occupied and lead you to the right path.

All major decisions require thinking skills. In order to become good problem-solvers, we must become good thinkers. All of our hurdles can be overcome through our minds. Sometimes we make issues bigger than they really are, simply by the way we think about them. If you think something will be difficult, it will be. If you think you can't overcome it, you won't! First, when approaching any major obstacle, look at it and tell yourself, "With God, I can do all things!" When you consider your problem to be solvable, it will be solved.

Before you make any major decisions, take time to do some reflective thinking. Think your problem through. Ask yourself questions like, "What will it take to overcome this hurdle?" "Will this help me accomplish my goals in life?" "How will this impact me?" and "What will this cost me?" Explore the "pros" and the "cons" of your actions. Then learn as much as you can in order to make an informed decision. Seek advice from others you trust, and conduct research, if necessary. When you gather all your facts, evaluate the cost of your proposed actions. If you feel confident after your evaluation, act upon your decision.

Make it a habit to always think things through. When you master this art, you will become an excellent thinker and problem-solver. Start today by fueling your mind with positive thoughts. Change your thinking and you will change your life!

Are you ready to deprogram your "stinking thinking" and reprogram your mind with "good thoughts?" If so, follow me in this prayer: *"God you are great, kind and merciful. Thank You for exposing me to the truth of the importance of my thinking. Today I desire to change my thoughts. Help me to uproot the negative thoughts that have adversely affected my mind. Help me to fill my mind with positive thoughts. Send positive people into my life who can support and encourage me. Alert me when my thoughts are off track, and help me to quickly change them. I thank You now for a new mind and the strength to sustain its purity. Amen."*

Congratulations, you have successfully completed this chapter. Now it is your job to evaluate your thinking. No longer allow negative thoughts to overcome your mind. Take control of such thoughts by kicking them out your mind! At first this may seem impossible, but as you catch yourself considering negative thoughts, change your thought patterns. Eventually you will develop the habit of positive thinking! As you pick up this habit, watch how your life will dramatically transform before your eyes. Good luck on your mission!

CHAPTER QUESTIONS

1) What is "stinking thinking?"
2) How did we develop our "stinking thinking?"
3) How can we now rid ourselves of our "stinking thinking?"
4) What is the law of attraction?
5) How do we attract good experiences into our lives?

WRITING ASSIGNMENT

Write down 10 negative thought patterns or misconceptions that you have developed in your lifetime. Then list the positive thoughts that you can now use to replace those negative thoughts.

CHAPTER 9

Managing Our Emotions

I n the last chapter, we learned the importance of positive thinking. We found that our thoughts dictate our actions, and that they also determine the way we feel. In this chapter, we will discover how we can use our thoughts to manage our emotions.

In our lives, many of us have learned how to react according to the way we feel. If we are angry, we may respond by screaming. If we are upset, we may begin to curse at someone. If we are threatened, we may start to fight. Life for many of us has been a series of learned reactions, rather than taking a logical approach to our problems.

As human beings we all have emotions. Emotions are our indicators that let us know how we should feel. Our feelings are important! They are the source of our joy, sadness, fear and anger. Our feelings allow us to laugh or to cry. They tell us if we are upset or if we fear because of danger. Our reactions are stimulated by our emotions.

Our emotions serve a good purpose in our lives, but we are not to be ruled solely by them. Our job is to manage and monitor our feelings prior to reacting to them. We must act as our own voices of reason. If we don't, emotions can lead us into a path of self-destruction. Many of us have been led onto the wrong path because we have failed to manage our feelings.

We have felt them and instantly reacted, not thinking of the consequences that lay behind our reaction. We have gone through life experiencing constant havoc because of poor choices that were stimulated by our emotions. Worse, many of us blame others for our reactions, rather than taking responsibility for them ourselves. Unfortunately we failed to understand that we do not have to react adversely to other people's bad behaviors. We have a choice. We can choose to manage our emotions!

Until we take control over our emotions, we will not be able to gain control over our lives. This chapter will examine in-depth the strategies we can use to take authority over our emotions.

The key to managing our emotions is to learn to control our thoughts. We spoke about this subject in the last chapter. The real battle takes place in our minds! We react according to how we perceive the events and circumstances that occur in our lives. When we begin to learn how to change and take dominion over our thoughts, we ultimately learn how to control our emotions. When we master our thinking, we master our emotions! This is a skill set that takes plenty of practice!

The emotions that we should be cautious of are negative emotions. They include fear, worry, doubt, depression, anger, hatred, anxiety, shame, guilt, greed, jealousy, and revenge. These emotions can all be relieved by simply removing negative thoughts from our minds and replacing them with positive thoughts. We do this by going to a quiet place and meditating. We can meditate by closing our eyes and bringing our minds to a peaceful state. In this state, we rid our minds of all negativity. We take ourselves, in our minds, to that peaceful place, and we envision ourselves being successful. In our meditation, we fill our minds with happy, peaceful, and positive thoughts. We take hold of these thoughts and keep them embedded in our minds. As we change our thoughts, we will notice the immediate change in our emotions. Instead of feeling a negative reaction, we will instantly feel more positive. It is this constant cleansing process that is necessary to maintain and control our emotions. When bad thoughts enter your thinking, you must consciously exchange them for more pleasant thoughts to ensure constant cleansing. This process is completed in meditation.

Anger is an emotion that we all feel from time to time. Anger can lead to both positive and negative results. Anger is positive when it signals to us that something is wrong or unjust. In this case, we are to feel the emotion, deal with the problem, and then let our anger go! Anger can also be a positive motivator to help us disconnect from unhealthy relationships in our lives. In this case, the energy of anger gives us the motivation we need to stand up for ourselves and detach.

When we hold onto or harbor anger within, it only produces undesirable results! Anger is released in raging, abusive, and manipulative behavior. Anger turned inward can produce depression, lack of motivation, self-abuse, and self-hatred. As we remain angry, we attract more angry situations into our lives, causing anger to destroy us.

Dealing properly with anger is a major problem for many of us. The abuse we have had to endure has built up inside, making us naturally angry people. When this occurs, and when we don't create a channel for it to be released, we repress our anger. Repressed anger is like a bomb waiting to go off. Many of us are walking bombshells. The smallest things can trigger a rage. This is not good! The consequences of our rage can be very costly. We have to learn to control our anger and diffuse it.

If we allow ourselves to become lost in anger, we can also become unable to feel our other emotions. Anger blocks us from being able to see the good that may come out of our everyday situations. Angry people view everything as bad. Anger dominates and overtakes our emotions until we address it, making it one of the most powerful emotions. Unresolved anger can also turn into resentment. Resentment is the feeling of grievance or ill-will towards another that lasts long after the situation that caused the original feeling is over. Unaddressed resentment eventually turns into hate. Resentment also leads to unforgiveness and bitterness, which block us from receiving our intended blessings.

Tremendous energy lies inside our anger. Anger can also be contagious. Reactive anger is when we get mad because someone else is mad. We easily pick up the feeling of another person, causing us to react in a way we never intended. Anger is so powerful that it makes it difficult to disperse the energy that it carries. Anger will not go away on its own, or by ignoring or repressing it. All anger must be dealt with! The only way to get rid of the energy that comes from anger is to learn how to re-channel it into as many healthy ways as we can. We can channel negative energy by practicing physical fitness, running, playing sports, writing about it, talking about it, or by doing any other activities that require intensive energy.

When the emotion of anger arises, we must give ourselves permission to feel angry. We must also give others permission to feel angry. Remember, anger is merely an emotion. It is not right or wrong to feel angry. The Bible says in Ephesians, Chapter 4, verses 26-27, "Be angry but sin not, do not let the sun go down on your anger." This lets us know that it's okay to feel this way, but it is not okay to act adversely because of these feelings. The scripture states, again, "Do not let the sun go down on your anger." That means feel the emotions of anger, then get rid of them. When we are angry, we must address it, deal with the emotion, and not go to sleep with angry feelings.

Now that we understand that it is okay to feel angry at times, we must learn how to manage the emotion of anger. When anger comes, allow yourself to feel it and any underlying emotions as well, such as hurt or fear. Acknowledge your thoughts as they come. Analyze them to see if your thinking is correct. Preferably, discuss your feelings with someone you trust, someone who is positive. Get their point of view about your situation as well. Then make a responsible decision about what actions you need to take, if any. Our job is to figure out what our anger is telling us. Is there a problem inside ourselves or in our environment that we need to address? Do we need to change ourselves within? Do we need help or support from someone? Our job is to properly assess each situation and to learn how to solve our problems correctly.

Screaming, yelling, and fighting never solve problems! They may temporarily diffuse an issue, but afterwards the problem still lingers on. Effective communication is the only way to solve problems in our relationships with others. We can easily resolve anger by figuring out what we need from the person with whom we are angry. Then we can ask that person for what we need. If he or she refuses to give it to us, then we can determine what we need to do next to take care of ourselves. This is the correct way to deal with anger in our lives. Stop spending unnecessary energy and time on issues that are not important. Detach from people that bring negative energy to you. Stick to the facts! Is this matter really important? If not, drop your anger and continue with your life. If it is important, will you get what you need out of the situation or from the person? If not, detach and move on. Refuse to let other people put their trash inside your can! If they do, quickly dump it and get on with your life! You have bigger issues to handle. Do not become stagnant or lose your focus. Keep your eyes on the prize!

If you find yourself being controlled by angry feelings, don't be discouraged. You still have the power to stop yourself. Change your environment if possible. Detach yourself and go to another room or another place. Get quiet and peaceful so you can examine your thoughts. Try your best to change your mood by changing your perception. What good can come out of this? What events led up to this? How can you get to the root of the problem? Are you overreacting? Analyze your thoughts, deal with your feelings, and then let them go!! Under no circumstances should you stay angry. Anger repressed will be more destructive to you than to the person who you are angry with. Do yourself a favor, and nip anger in the bud!

Addressing our anger has allowed us to sharpen our problem-solving skills. Remember, we will all have problems in life. The issue is how we address those problems and how we deal with them. We are to always look for the good in every situation and to view matters as well from the other parties' perspective. Life isn't all about us. It is about others too! Sometimes our actions and behaviors provoke people to act as they do. Along with monitoring our emotions and feelings, we need to monitor our actions and behavior patterns. We must make it a priority to consider others. When we take others into account, not only do we make circumstances more peaceful for them, but we also benefit. Other people will become more pleasant to us, especially when they see that we also have their best interests at heart. How can we operate daily, taking care of our own needs, but also being mindful of others? This should become our priority. When we activate this principle in our lives, it will make life's course a lot smoother.

Another group of negative emotions that can affect us adversely are fear, worry, and doubt. These powerful emotions can paralyze us! Fear of the unknown keeps us stuck in the cycles with which we are comfortable. They stop us from venturing outside familiar territory, making it hard to achieve our dreams. The acronym for fear is "False Evidence Appearing Real." We must not fear anything or anyone except God. When we make the correct choices in life, we are protected. God will always provide for us and keep us from hurt, harm, and danger. Fear should never be an option for us.

Fear is tormenting. When we allow it to come into our lives, we become flooded with more fear. Remember the law of attraction. Whatever we think or believe, we attract more of it into our lives. That's why it is important to quickly discard fear.

We cannot live victoriously while we are trapped in fear, because we will then be afraid to accomplish our goals and purpose in life. Based on a false precept, fear is ultimately a lie! It is a tactic used by the enemy to keep us in bondage. We must overcome fear by embracing the unknown with our faith, knowing that good will come out of every situation when we pass the test. The test is to recognize the purpose or the good in every obstacle that life brings. When we live an integral lifestyle and do what is right, whether anyone is watching or not, we will begin to live in peace, not fear.

A worried or a doubtful mind produces nothing good. It keeps us in a state of confusion, which makes it difficult for us to make clear decisions or choices. When we are confused, we cannot operate at our full potential. We need to remain confident, knowing that everything is going to work out in our favor!

Many of us spend a lot of our time worrying. Worrying is negative meditation. It is constantly thinking about the "What if?" and what can go wrong. When we place our attention on our fears, it gives them the energy to manifest their outcome in our lives. Worrying and doubting are tormenting and allow no room for peace. Instead, they constantly rattle our emotions. When we make choices or decisions in a fearful state, we are more likely to make the wrong decisions. These emotions can motivate us to do the wrong thing, even when we want to do the right thing. Do not let yourself be motivated by fear, worry, or doubt. When you detect these emotions, quickly eliminate them.

When we allow negative emotions to take root, such as fear, worry and doubt, we are saying to God by our actions that we do not trust Him. We conquer these emotions by having faith, resting in the fact that we know our "Higher Power" has got our back. We have made it this far, and He's able to see us through the rest of the journey.

We rid ourselves of negative emotions by changing our thoughts. We have to train our minds that we are God's wonderful creations. As a result, we will receive God's best for our lives. Wonderful things will happen to us! When undesirable events occur, there is always a good purpose. Something good will come out of every situation! In the end, all things will work together for our good. Once we embed these positive ideas into our minds, we will be able to function in peace and joy. Our inner peace and joy will direct the universe to send us an abundance of good experiences.

Remember, regardless of your situation and what you are going through, no matter how bad it may seem, stay rooted in positive thoughts. Let nothing and no one steal your joy, regardless of what comes your way! Those that are able to endure will become the winners in life. They are the ones who will ultimately receive the prize! You are the only one who has the power to label your experiences. If you call an event bad, it will be bad. If you label an event good, you will find the good in your experience. Life is about your perspective: If you don't like the hand life has dealt you, change your perspective on it.

The only way to keep our vision clear and our emotions controlled is to constantly pray and meditate. When we are faced with situations beyond our control, we must turn them over to God. Prayer and meditation are our sources of communication with Him. We speak to God by becoming quiet and peaceful. We erase everything from our minds and give Him our complete focus. We can pray out loud to God, or we can pray silently, which is called meditation. Meditation and prayer release us from the heavy burdens of life that we don't need to carry. We relinquish our power and ask God for His wisdom, knowledge, and strength. God is faithful! When we ask and believe He has provided, we receive what we ask. If we do not ask, we will not receive! Also, if we do not believe, we will not receive from God! We have to position ourselves to stand before God with expectation. We must expect God to deliver our request when we come to Him with the correct heart and intent.

This chapter has dealt with the issues many of us have faced concerning our emotions. Dealing with our emotions will not be a simple or an easy process. It will take time to develop this skill set. We must become masters of our thoughts, a process that takes extensive mental training. At times we will do great, and other times, we may begin to slip, allowing negative thoughts to return. When you recognize those unhappy feelings approaching, that is your signal to change your thoughts. Regroup and change your thinking immediately, and you will sustain your peace.

Before you start your day and before you go to sleep, make it a habit to clear your mind and filter your thoughts. Many people like to read daily meditations in the morning. This is a good practice. It helps us to focus on the positive, which will help us start our day off right. How we begin our day is generally how we will finish it. Before you get out of bed, visualize yourself in your mind successfully accomplishing everything you need to do that day. At the end of the day, before you sleep, recap the events of the day. Acknowledge what you did right, and congratulate yourself! Also acknowledge what you did wrong. Think of what you need to do to fix those things that went wrong, then visualize in your mind doing that. Lastly, but most importantly, dump out all the trash of negative emotions! Immerse yourself with peaceful, happy thoughts. This process will help you sustain more pleasurable days as well as peaceful nights.

Learning to manage your emotions represents a huge step forward. When we conquer this principle, we can conquer any obstacle life may bring us! There are great rewards to those who master this art. Are you ready to become the master of your thoughts and emotions? If so, follow me in this prayer: *"God, I thank You for exposing to me the importance of managing my emotions. I come to You today seeking Your help, strength, and guidance. Enable me to learn how to control my emotions. Guide me with Your wisdom. Help me to see Your purpose and plan for my life. Illuminate the good in every situation. Allow me to see it and reflect on it in my thinking, regardless of what I am experiencing. Shower down Your love upon me and erase all my fears, worries and doubts. Show me my strengths, gifts and talents, and give me the confidence I need to obtain my goals and my purpose in life. Keep me protected from all evil, hurt, and harm. Shine Your light upon me. Transform my heart and mind, and lead me into Your expected results. Amen."*

Now that we have completed this prayer, we have the strength we need to monitor our thoughts, emotions, and feelings. Pause throughout the day to take an assessment of your thoughts. Refuse to allow destructive thoughts to take root in your mind, Begin to read books that reflect on the positive. Check out the bibliography list in the back of this book, and choose some positive books to read. If you want to improve yourself, you must work on your mind first. When you begin to develop good mental habits, watch how quickly your life will change for the good. Good luck on your journey, you are well on your way to victory.

CHAPTER QUESTIONS

1) Why are our emotions important? Why are our thoughts important?
2) Name 3 positive emotions and 3 negative emotions.
3) How can we manage our emotions?
4) How can anger be a positive motivator? How can anger be a negative motivator?
5) How can we infuse positive emotions into our experiences?

WRITING ASSIGNMENT

Keep a daily log of your feelings for one week. When you feel positive emotions, write them down and describe how you feel. Analyze why you're feeling this way. What happened to give you those emotions? Also, make a record of when you feel negative emotions. Write down the emotions and describe how you feel. Analyze what triggered these emotions. When you are finished, review your log and analyze how your emotions affected you. Then, list three ways you can diffuse your negative emotions and three ways you can sustain your positive emotions for longer periods of time.

CHAPTER 10

Learning to Care for "Self"

In Chapter 3 we discussed the detriment of many of us being caught up in society's perceptions of what's good and what's bad, what's "hot" and what's "not." Many have spent several years chasing unrealistic, and at times unethical, standards in order to be accepted by others. In this chase, many of us have lost touch with our "true self." We don't know who we really are and what we really like, because we are so consumed by being the person we believe others will like. We wear masks, and give the illusion to others that we are happy. Unfortunately, deep down inside, we are empty. Feeling defeated, we unconsciously or consciously view our true "self" as less than acceptable. For many, this thinking has turned into self-hate, which is one of the most destructive emotions. Projected outward, it becomes violence, war, crime, and oppression. Sadly, many of us are in our current dilemmas because of our own self-hate. Deep down we don't love ourselves; if we did, we would have never allowed our "self" to make the many undesirable decisions that have ultimately jeopardized our well-being. We have become so driven in the chase of life that we have forgotten and neglected that which is most important — our "self."

In this chapter, we will learn the importance of "self" and how to take care of "self." We will work intensely on re-building our broken self-esteem. In that effort, we will come to understand how to implement new "self" care techniques, which will help us to improve our lives and reach our maximum potential.

Success and happiness start from within. In order to overcome the challenges and the obstacles that lie ahead, we must work on "self." When our "self" changes, our circumstances will ultimately change as well. The root of our problems has stemmed from our perception of "self." It is now time for us to discard every ounce of self-hate and accept and love our "self" wholeheartedly. As we fall in love with "self," the world will begin to embrace us as well. It's time to get in touch with "self," and to know whom we truly are. Each of us must recognize our own likes and dislikes. We must not be influenced by the views of others. There is an old saying, "Different strokes for different folks." We have to learn that it is okay to be who we are. We are only obligated to be the best "self" we can be!

Contrary to how you may think or feel in your current state, you are beautiful. God uniquely created you and designed you after His own image. He shaped you and molded you with your personality and your own unique talents and gifts with His plan for your life in mind. Stop comparing yourself to others, and measuring your self-worth based on someone else's standards. You are special and unique! I personally admire your strength. The average person could never have endured all that you have experienced and still be standing strong. You are indeed a warrior! You have so many gifts and talents that you haven't even tapped into yet. Use this time to discover all that lies dormant inside. Develop these talents and go home ahead of the game. You can and will be happy and successful! Your only job is to tap into your greater "self," which is you at your fullest potential. Stop settling for mediocrity; there's nothing regular about you.

Regular people don't take the risks you have taken in life. The risk-takers are the most successful people in the world. Now use your bold audacity in a positive way. Fearlessly, remove the chains of bondage that have held you down for so long. Erase from your mind all the lies the enemy has told you. Stop feeling sorry for yourself! Life isn't over! Dust the defilement off your shoulders, and take all the energy you have inside and redirect it to focus on becoming successful.

Close your eyes and imagine yourself in your dream job. Imagine leaving work and jumping into your dream car. Turn on the CD player and pop in your favorite song. Listen to it playing as you head down the road in your new car. As you are driving, admire the scenery of your new neighborhood. Wave at your neighbors and honk the horn. See how friendly they are? Pull up on your block and pull into the driveway of your dream home. Open the door with your keys and look around. Your family members are inside to greet you and to let you know how proud they are of you. Can you visualize that picture? Do you feel that happiness and joy? Hold on to that picture in your mind. When times get rough and you're having a bad day, close your eyes and recap that image. Before you get up in the morning and before you close your eyes at night, hold on to that vision. See it, believe that it will be your future, and it will be yours! You can have whatever you set your mind to achieve. The question is, do you really want it? If so, roll up your sleeves and let's get to work on the biggest asset that can make it all happen: "self."

In order to reach your goals in life, you have to believe in your "self." To develop this belief, you must learn how to fall in love with "self." This process begins by nurturing "self." Nurturing is the means we use to empower and energize "self." Nurturing is an attitude toward "self" of unconditional love and acceptance. In the morning and throughout our day, we must lovingly and gently ask "self" what can we do for "self" that will feel good, and what do we need to do to take care of "self?" When we are hurt, we need to ask what will help us feel better? When we are down, we must give "self" encouragement and support. When we take on challenging tasks, we can tell our "self," "You can do it!" This is the way we nurture "self." Inevitably, we form the habit of doing wonderful things for "self" that we wish someone else would have done for us. We don't wait for happiness, we take it!

Our job is to become our own lover, best friend, and parent. We must unconditionally love "self," regardless of our faults. Instead of criticizing "self," we must seek out avenues to improve "self." Love your "self" in order to return to a state of wholeness. Be patient with "self," and never critical. When you make a mistake, tell "self" it's okay. Ask "self" if there something you can learn from this mistake. Learn the lesson and discard the feelings of guilt and shame. Refuse to accept unearned guilt and shame. Guard "self" from those feelings of inadequacy. Make a commitment to "self" that you will always protect it and look out for the best interests of "self." Don't allow "self" to be in a position to be harmed or in danger. Never jeopardize "self!"

When we begin to fall in love with, and care for "self" with kindness and compassion, that's when we truly become whole. Many of us have been looking for people, places and things to complete us. We believed we needed these elements to make us happy and fulfilled. This has been one of our biggest mistakes! We must take care of our "self," and begin to control how we feel. We cannot allow others to control our emotions!

In Chapter 3, we spoke about codependency, which is essentially depending on others to make us happy and fulfilled. Many of us have based our lives on catering to others, with the hopes of making them happy, so that they will make us happy. In many cases, it has backfired on us, because no person has the ability to fulfill you. They can temporary enhance your happiness, but the control lies in their hands and they decide when and if they will act. No person should ever have such control over you!

When we are not complete and we enter relationships with the expectation that another person will complete us, nothing good can come from those relationships. Our relationships will be a constant roller coaster, going up and down based on the other person's feelings. We learned in the last chapter how to control our emotions, which is a key ingredient to becoming whole. When we don't know how to take charge of our emotions, we take the baggage of unnecessary reactions to our feelings into our relationships, and ultimately we destroy what could have been a good relationship. Fixing our "self" is all about wholeness. As we work on the areas of our lives that need improvement, we are caring for "self." When our "self" is whole, we will be complete and fulfilled. Now is the time for us to get to know "self" and the needs of "self."

Have you ever taken the time to sit down and decide what you like and what you dislike? What brings you joy? What do you do that makes you feel good about "self?" What are your favorite meals? What are your favorite hobbies and activities? What do you like to do to reward yourself? What are your favorite places? What are your biggest fears? What makes you sad? What makes you feel unsafe? Take out your *Voices of Consequences, "Unlocking the Prison Doors"* Workbook/Journal and answer these questions. Take your time and think about them. Give your honest answers and don't let them be based on the views of others. Think about "self" and what you can do to make "self" happy. Complete this exercise, and then return to this chapter.

Now that you are discovering the things that satisfy you, you must begin to make it a constant practice to care and pamper your "self" as much as you can. As you do this, you will begin to increase your self-esteem. Remember the law of attraction: *like attracts like.* As we begin to treat our "self" like the queen that she is, we will send the energy of love and care towards "self" into the universe. This energy will propel back to us the energy of others who will also begin to treat us as we treat ourselves.

Have you ever noticed a woman who, on the outside, didn't seem very attractive, yet she possessed an attitude that said she was "that chick?" I even recall a song of a female rapper whose hook stated, "I'm conceited and I have a reason." These women put the energy of self-confidence into the universe, where others pick it up and treat them accordingly. You and I may say, "How in the world did she get him to like her?" It all started with her confidence and appreciation of "self." When we love and respect ourselves, our energy will demand love and respect in return.

Many of us have spent our lives as caretakers to others. We have been so worried about pleasing others in order to gain their acceptance, that we have forgotten about "self." Each person is responsible for her "self." Our job is not to take care of any individual except our children, and perhaps immediate family members. When we take on responsibilities for others, we "disable" them. This can be dangerous! As a result, that person no longer relies on himself, but rather begins to rely on you. Instead of using your energy to work on you, you are left to exert your energy working on the other person. This is unhealthy for both you and the other person!

"Self"-care is an attitude of mutual respect. It means that we learn to live our lives in a responsible manner. It also means that we allow others to live their lives as they choose, as long as they don't interfere with our decisions to live our lives as we choose. "Self"-care means that we understand our needs are important, so we address them. Our needs become our first priority. We lose our low self-worth and self-esteem as we learn to see the beauty that lies in "self." We begin to think independently and to make choices that are good for "self." We know what we think, what we feel, what we need, what we desire, and we acknowledge our right to experience our feelings. We learn to accept who we are, and we speak and express our true feelings. We are loyal to "self," which eventually produces "self"-love. As a result, we fall in love with our own life, our own purpose, and our own potential. We no longer stand in awe of others. We begin to stand in awe of "self!"

Taking care of "self" is not about being selfish. It is about being responsible. We still give to others and show them compassion, yet we learn to be responsible in our giving. The Bible says, "Love thy neighbor as thyself," which means that we are not to put people above ourselves. This is a common mistake that many of us have made in our past. We have put everything and everyone before "self," and now look at the position we are in! Where are all the people whom we cared for so passionately? This time around, we must learn to care for "self." When we master this art then we can extend our hand of friendship to others, because only then will we know how to be a true friend. Our relationships require boundaries. Without boundaries, there is no order and chaos reigns.

Boundaries in relationships draw the line between what we will and will not tolerate. All good relationships have boundaries. Boundaries let us know how far to let people go. When they cross the line, we do what's necessary to stop them, and we protect our "self." In our relationships, we should no longer be willing to sacrifice our self-esteem, self-respect, our children's well being, our jobs, homes, freedom, possessions, safety, credit, sanity, or ourselves in order to preserve a relationship. Therefore, we choose to create boundaries that ensure our safety. When we recognize that any of these boundaries are jeopardized, we do what's necessary to remove ourselves from the relationship. We no longer have to be willing to lose everything in the name of "love." Real love gives; it doesn't take away! When we learn to care for "self," we establish what we are willing to give to another by creating boundaries. We have the choice to protect ourselves, our time, our talents and our money. Boundaries don't complicate our lives, they simplify them. They mean we stop taking care of others and their feelings, and we take care of our "self."

When we begin to set boundaries, we must be sincere and firm. Our "yes" must mean "yes" and our "no" must mean "no." When we compromise our boundaries, they are no longer valid. People will not take us seriously and they will begin to abuse us. We protect "self" when we mean what we say! We don't disrespect ourselves, nor do we allow anyone else to take advantage of us. Instead, we confidently stand firm as our own protector.

As we begin to develop healthy boundaries, we will develop appropriate roles for friends, family members, others, and ourselves. We learn to respect others, their space, and their choices as we learn to respect ourselves. We don't use or abuse others, nor do we allow them to abuse us! We stop taking responsibility for others, and we learn to take responsibility for ourselves. As we develop such parameters, we begin to feel good about ourselves. We no longer just settle, nor do we allow ourselves to be mistreated. We take a stand for ourselves! This new stance brings us a new value of "self"-worth.

Setting boundaries is an ongoing process that requires constant work. We must learn to listen to our inner desires and our needs. We must ask ourselves, "What hurts?" We stop to hear the lesson in our pain. Then we ask ourselves, "What feels good?" And we make it our job to ensure that our "self" is happy and safe. Setting boundaries creates the basis for respecting "self." The more we respect ourselves, the more others will begin to respect us.

Taking care of "self" also includes health and grooming. When we don't look good, it is hard to feel good about "self." We can no longer afford to deprive our "self." Even in prison, take care of your "self." Iron your uniform; get your hair done at hair care. Look your best, not for anyone else, but for yourself. Make up your face and look in the mirror. Smile at yourself and tell yourself, "You are beautiful." As you do these things, you will build your self-esteem. Your energy then radiates into the universe, shouting "She loves herself." When this happens, others will begin to love and admire you, too. Health and grooming in prison does matter! Take care of yourself!

In order to maintain proper health, watch your diet and exercise. Don't mistreat your body. Exercising allows us to stay in shape. It helps us to look good and to feel good about ourselves, simply by taking the time to care for "self." We can start by walking around the neighborhood, or walking the track and field. We can play a sport, take an exercise class, or work out in the gym. As we do, we will feel a sense of "self"-appreciation. As we begin to feel good about ourselves, we develop the self-esteem we need to achieve our goals in life.

Caring for "self" also includes "self"-development. We need to take the time to understand our purpose, and what we want to accomplish in life. As we set goals and work diligently to achieve them, we are also caring for "self." The second book in the *Voices of Consequences Enrichment Series, Permission to Dream* will help us develop our talents and skill sets so we can reach our dreams. As we improve our "self," we improve our lives!

It's time to take a stand! We must stop reacting to other people's dysfunction and remove ourselves from circumstances where we are the victim. We must also stop punishing ourselves for other people's problems, and stop expecting others to satisfy our needs! We must care for "self" and learn how to satisfy "self." As we decrease our expectation in people, places, and things, and increase our expectation in "self," we will tap into the potential that lies dormant within.

Are you ready to start the habit of caring for "self?" If so, then follow me in this prayer: *"God, I thank You for showing me the beauty and the importance of 'self.' I ask that You help me to recognize my full potential that lies within. Empower me to see myself from Your perspective. Teach me how to love, care, and appreciate 'self.' When I fall short in these areas, gently nudge me and remind me to care for 'self.' Give me the strength I need to sustain that care. Increase my self-esteem and confidence daily as I embark on this journey of restoration. Lead me and guide me into Your perfect will and plan. Amen."*

You have just completed one of the most important chapters in this entire series. It's so important that we practice caring for "self." Review this chapter several times until you are able to grasp these techniques and principles, and apply them to your life. Change starts with "self." As you value "self," life will begin to value you! Good luck on your journey.

CHAPTER QUESTIONS
1) What is caring for "self?"
2) How do we care for "self?"
3) What are boundaries?
4) Why do we need boundaries to maintain healthy relationships?

5) Why is it important to maintain proper health and grooming, even in prison?

WRITING ASSIGNMENT

From the list you created of your likes and dislikes, write an affirmation that details how you will begin to daily care for "self." Start off your affirmation as follows: Today is a new day. Today I have learned the value of "self." I love and appreciate my "self," therefore I will (*fill in the blanks*).

UNLOCKING THE PRISON DOORS

CHAPTER 11
Alternatives to Crime

There comes a point in our lives where we must put away our childish ways and become responsible. Instead of simply living for today, we must keep tomorrow in mind. In our choices, we must consider our future. All crime comes with consequences, whether it is immediate or in the future. We can no longer jeopardize our future by continuing to commit crimes. We will know when we have reached maturity: Mature adults make responsible decisions! Mature adults are unwilling to risk harm or danger to themselves. Have you reached maturity?

Many of us have chosen to live criminal lifestyles because we were looking for instant results. Just as quickly as we gained results, we lost them! We took two steps forward and three steps back. When you weigh the "pros" and "cons" of living a criminal lifestyle, the math does not add up. We would have been better off slowing down, taking our time and building a foundation that would last! Success requires sacrifice. You have to give up something to gain something, but the gains that come with responsible behavior are long lasting and make it all worth it. Many of us are back at the beginning. We have to rebuild our foundation in order to build our new house. The foundation is the most important part of the house. If it is not solid, the whole house will collapse! Many of us have built fabulous houses in our past, yet when the storm came, the house went tumbling down. Why? It fell because the house was not built on a strong foundation. Our new foundation must be built on sound principles and integrity, which requires hard work. Short cuts will always result in failure, so we must avoid them at all cost!

Being in a prison, we have a tremendous amount of free time to think about what we want to do in life. Instead of being influenced by others, we need to decide what we like to do, and what we do well that others find difficult to do. When we find these answers, we will be headed on the path of purpose. The next book in this series, entitled *Permission to Dream*, will help us tap into our purpose. In the meantime, let's prepare our minds to discover the unique talents and abilities we each have. As we begin to concentrate and work on our strengths, we will begin to improve "self." What do you excel at doing? What can you do for extensive periods of time without becoming bored? What activities can you do that keep your adrenaline pumping?

It's time to tap into your greater "self." That is your skill set that makes you special and unique from others. When you find these skill sets, your job is to strengthen and develop them. Instead of focusing on what your faults are, focus on your strengths.

Many of us were involved in crimes that involved special skills. At the time we were committing the crimes we were unaware of the skill sets we possessed. In order to make money and do it successfully, you need a skill. Go back and analyze your crime and take note of the skills you had to successfully pull off your crime. Then determine how you can take the same abilities and make legitimate money using them.

EXAMPLE #1

I grew up in Queens, NY around many drug dealers and hustlers. They had the skill set of selling. Many of them had the "gift of gab," as we called it, or the ability to sell. In the early 2000s, the drug trade started to slow in our neighborhood. The cops were hot on the blocks, and the boys started to figure out that the consequences of their crime far outweighed the gain, so many of them went out of state to sell drugs. Others tried new ventures. The new hustle was to go to lower Manhattan, to the garment district, and buy t-shirts and socks wholesale, and bring them back to the neighborhood to sell them. Surprisingly to the boys, they began to make more money selling t-shirts and socks than they did selling drugs. How were they able to accomplish this? The boys had developed excellent sales skills and techniques while they were out on the block trying to convince dope fiends to buy drugs from them. They utilized these same skill sets to sell their t-shirts and socks. As a result, they had the entire neighborhood buying clothes from them! One of the boys was smart enough to set up a little store in the neighborhood and others also began to redirect their skills in a positive direction. Some became real estate sales agents and sales executives for large firms. Their employers realized they had a keen knack for sales, but they had no clue how they gained it. It was all courtesy of the late nights grinding on the block and the creative tactics these boys used to sell their drugs. They were able to flip and use their talents legitimately! They are no different from you and I. Let's take what we have, dust it off, and refine it. Then we can use it for good.

EXAMPLE #2

I grew up in the same neighborhood as DJ Clue – a well-known Hip-Hop deejay. My brother and Clue were very good friends, and I watched Clue come up from nothing. The boys were very mischievous in the street, yet Clue tapped into his talent. He watched another deejay in our area, "Baby Jay," at parties, and Clue said to himself, "I can do that, too!" At first he was greatly criticized. Everyone felt he was trying to be like Baby Jay. They both sold mixed tapes at that time in the

137

neighborhood, and Baby Jay sold more mixed tapes than Clue. Clue was probably not more talented than Baby Jay at the time, but Clue had better business skills. Clue began to create logos to market his product, and he expanded outside of Queens to the surrounding boroughs. Within his first couple of years in the business, DJ Clue far surpassed Baby Jay. Today you can see his CDs in every mix tape store throughout the country, and even in major record stores. Why? Clue had passion. He knew what he wanted, and he was smart enough to create strategic tactics to surpass his competition. He is no different from you and I! He took his talent, focused on it, and made it his strength!

EXAMPLE #3

My daughter's aunt Jessica is another woman who tapped into her talent and purpose. She grew up in the Roosevelt housing projects in Brooklyn, NY, where she was a regular "hood chick." She graduated from high school and had a son named Malik. She wanted a better life for herself, but she wasn't sure how to get it. One day she went to one of the local hospitals to look for a job. She had minimal skills and no training, so she accepted an entry level position. The job paid very little, but it had excellent benefits. She worked her way up from department to department, and she took advantage of the hospital's tuition reimbursement program. Ten years later, she is still working at the same hospital, but now as a registered nurse. Her schooling was funded by the hospital, and she is now working towards becoming a doctor. What an accomplishment for the little girl who grew up in the hood with very little money. She was a struggling single mother who took advantage of an opportunity. Now she is happily married and lives very comfortably. She is no different than you and I !

EXAMPLE #4

I have another friend named Chrisilie Tillerson. She was born and raised in Detroit, Michigan. Chrisilie grew up in a rough neighborhood, and her mother was heavily addicted to drugs. One of the local drug dealers gave Chrisilie's mother some drugs on consignment, and her mother did not pay him back on time. The boy began to harass her mother and even attempted to cause her mother bodily harm. Chrisilie eventually tried to protect her mother and ended up with a murder charge. She received a 10-year sentence, and she served 7 years.

Chrisilie came home focused and on a mission to make up for lost time. She enrolled in an entrepreneur program in Detroit for ex-felons. She passionately pursued her dream of owning her own trucking company. She completed the course and found a mentor who was seasoned in the field. Chrisilie was able to use state grant money to buy her first truck, and her future began there. Chrisilie today is very successful! She owns one of the top ranking minority transportation companies in the Detroit area. She is no different than you and I! She found her talent, and she found state funding to help her cause. Today she benefits from her persistence. She accomplished her dream!

Did you know Don King is an ex-felon? He served several years in jail for murder. Today he is one of the greatest and richest promoters ever. Why? He found his talent and passion and he pursued it! He is no different than you and I!

Malcolm X was also an ex-felon. He spent his time in jail reading and researching. In jail he took the time out to work on "self," he came home and quickly excelled. He even made history! Malcolm X is no different than you and I !

I share these stories with you because I want you to understand life doesn't end here. This is where it begins!

We have a point to prove. The point is we can make it, regardless of what others have said or what they think about us. This time around, we are going to beat the odds! We are going to show them what we are made of!

I want you to consider what you'd like to do after incarceration. Together, we are going to create a plan that you can follow that will help you to achieve success. I want you to start reading books about the profession you are considering . Do some research and talk to others, so you can gather the information needed to determine what it will take to achieve this goal.

While imprisoned, visit the prison's resource center or write your state office to learn about the programs they have available for ex-convicts. There are millions of dollars that the state and federal government allot each year to felons. Many grants and other funds are not tapped into because of lack of knowledge. Former President George Bush enacted the Second Chance Act, which most think is just for getting out of prison early. This Act has several funding areas for ex-felons. Read the entire Act and find out what funding may apply to you.

Some of us are going to have to swallow our pride and get state or government assistance. I have a girlfriend who was homeless. She moved into a shelter with her two little children. The shelter helped her find her own apartment, and she was able to qualify for Section 8. She received public assistance while they paid for her to go to college. She also completed a course in money management offered by the state, which gave her a grant to purchase a $5000 car. She utilized all the resources available and completed her education. Today she is very successful in her trade. She is no different than you and I! She swallowed her pride, sacrificed a little, and now she is set for life!

Transition may not be easy, but the ones who endure will become successful. Whatever we do, we cannot look back! We've done enough damage. Focus and be smart! Let's use our gifts and talents this time in a positive way. Remember, you may have to sacrifice. Landing your dream job with a felony may not be easy, but nothing is impossible! You may have to take that entry level position like Jessica did and work your way up to the top. You may even have to volunteer your services to get through the door, but it's okay! Whenever you do get your shot, make sure you shine! Let them see that there's no one who can do quite what you do the way you do it. Be dependable! Be courteous! Work diligently! You will be recognized and promoted! Never give up and never turn back! Always continue to improve "self." As you continue to work on "self," you will continue to excel in life. Whatever trade you choose, study as much as you can about that field. Learn all ins and outs and become educated! Promotion comes in life when we gain wisdom and knowledge.

Being an ex-con comes with a negative stigma, but we can overcome that stigma once we allow our light to shine. Show the world you are not the typical ex-con, and you are determined. It is your determination that will make you successful!

The Voices of Consequences Enrichment Series was created to assist you in improving "self" and transitioning successfully back into the free world. If you are serious about changing your life and want to take the correct path, this is the series for you! Don't stop after reading this book. Continue and complete the entire series, which consists of six books in total accompanied by a daily meditation book. Use this time wisely. Improve your greatest asset, "self." Your hard work and persistence will pay off! You will receive the wisdom and knowledge you need to get ahead in life.

Let's close this chapter with a short prayer: *"God, I thank You for opening my mind to alternatives to crime. I deeply desire to change my old ways and habits. I ask for Your guidance along this journey. Help me to discover my gifts and talents. Illuminate the areas that I am strongest in. Send me people and resources that will promote my cause. Keep me from all evil and temptation. Help me to stay focused on my goals and not be distracted or go off track. I thank You now for Your wisdom, knowledge and direction. Amen."*

CHAPTER QUESTIONS
1) Why must we give up our lifestyle of crime?
2) Why is it important to discover our skills and talents?
3) How can we overcome the stigma of being an ex-con?
4) In which ways can we discover more information about the field we wish to study, or the occupation we want to pursue?
5) Why are shortcuts dangerous?

WRITING ASSIGNMENT
Write down what you would like to pursue as an occupation after prison. Describe what steps you will have to take to accomplish this goal. Explain what you can do now in prison that will prepare you for this experience.

CHAPTER 12

Each Day Becoming a Better "Self"

W e've come a long way in a short period of time. In this book we've covered a vast array of topics concerning improving "self." In this chapter, we will review the key techniques and strategies we have learned. We will take these different techniques and learn how to apply them to our lives. Our goal is to turn these techniques into our daily habits. When they become habits, we will instinctively begin to apply them to our lives, and we will become a better "self."

Each of us is a work in progress. Change will not occur overnight! It will take time, hard work, and dedication, but the results are well worth it! Change starts with the redirection of our minds. As we change our mindset, our focus will change, and we will be uplifted. Whatever we focus on, we can and will accomplish! It's time to focus on improving "self." We need to determine what our desired results are and direct our focus toward the finished product.

In this book, we determined our strengths and our weaknesses. Now, we need to diligently work on improving our weaknesses. Then we can focus on improving our strengths. When we tap into our strengths and become even better in these areas, we will begin to soar! We are all unique individuals. No one is quite like us. When we discover our purpose and tap into our gifts, our light will begin to shine brightly for the world to see. Our goal is to find the light within. When we turn on this light, it will quickly dispel the darkness that has tried to overtake us. The key is to find the light switch within! We achieve this by caring, discovering, and improving "self." What are you waiting for? Turn on the light!

Today marks a brand new day! Don't delay! Immediately implement the new techniques we have learned. We must start before we open our eyes in the morning. We give thanks to God for allowing us to see another day, and we ask Him to lead us and guide us into a perfect day. Then we review in our minds all that we need to accomplish that day. We see ourselves vividly succeeding in accomplishing those tasks, peacefully and happily. We feel the satisfaction of having moved through our day productively. After we experience our day successfully in our mind, we get up and prepare to start the day. As we approach the bathroom mirror to comb our hair and brush our teeth, we look in the mirror and greet our "self." We say, "Self, I love you. You are so beautiful. I appreciate you, so today I will protect you. I will do my best to make sure you feel loved and appreciated. You are very special to me." As we say these words with sincere feelings of admiration and appreciation, we will begin to feel good about "self." We complete the necessary tasks to start our day, but before we begin our regular activities, we must first read a daily meditation. This can be from any empowering author. I recommend that you read, *Making the Best out of Time*, which is part of the *Voices of Consequences Enrichment Series*. It is a daily meditation book that gives you a couple of paragraphs to read each day to uplift you and cause you to focus on "self." You can also read the *Daily Bread*, which is a Christian devotional that you can find at the prison chapel, or some excerpts out of the Bible, or excerpts from your own religious books. Whatever you read, make sure it is inspirational and uplifting — words that you can meditate on and ponder throughout your day.

If you complete this task each morning, before you start your day, you will witness incredible positive results! You are commanding your day by applying these techniques, which means that you are taking control over what you will and will not allow during this day. Remember, the mind is very powerful! We get back the energy we disperse. When you start your day off positively in your mind, you are radiating strong energy to bring you positive results outwardly.

After you are out the door, whether you are driving or walking to your destination, use this time to consider who you wish to be. See yourself in the final results, as we discussed earlier. Experience the joy you will feel when you achieve your dream. The energy you derive from your futuristic visualization will help you transition through your day, and it will give your day purpose! You now know that in order to get where you intend to go in life, you must get through this day. This sense of purpose will allow you to bear any pain or obstacles that may come. We stand and we endure because we know we have a plan. Our hard work and our endurance are not in vain! We move forward with energy and the assurance that this day will pay off in our future.

Whenever you experience difficulties throughout the day, go back to the picture you created in your visualization. It will help spark energy even in the midst of your adverse circumstances. It is the hidden instrument you can use any time you feel depressed. When you focus on the prize, or the end result, you'll have all the energy you need to maintain your momentum.

As you move along through your day, check your feelings. If you are feeling down, that is your indicator that you have allowed yourself to take in negative thoughts. Stop and remove all negative ideas and concepts. Then, input happy, pleasant thoughts into your mind. Close your eyes for a moment. See yourself in a peaceful place. Lie on the "beach sand," on top of your blanket. Listen to the sounds of the water lapping up over the sand. Silently ask your "Higher Power" to help you remove all negative thoughts and energy, and ask Him to fill you with His presence. Once you disperse your negative thoughts, ask yourself, "What can I do to take care of you?" Think about the answer, and do what's necessary to maintain your peace.

Regardless if you are at home, work, or running errands, you must remain happy and joyous. Find ways to pass the day and accomplish your goals, but still have fun doing it. Listen to music that you enjoy. Think about special moments in your life. Relax and enjoy your day! Let nothing or no one steal your peace. If you are at work, find ways to make your job fun and enjoyable while you work. Create new strategies of accomplishing your task, or interact with your fellow employees in a joyous manner. Take control over your day, and don't let it control you!

If you encounter an obstacle, stop and think before you react. Ask yourself the question, "What good can come out of this situation?" Then take the time to find the good in it. Whatever you do, don't allow yourself to become upset and frustrated. Ask yourself, "What can I do to improve this situation?" and "What do I need to do to take care of 'self'?" After you find the answers, do your best to move through your obstacle.

If you make a mistake, immediately admit your error and take responsibility. Do what you need to do to move forward. Don't beat yourself up. Just learn from the lesson. Ask yourself the question, "What can I do to insure that I don't make the same mistake again?" Take note of the answer and proceed forward. Do not hold on to unnecessary shame and guilt! Forgive yourself and move on.

146

If you find yourself coming in contact with someone who is difficult to deal with, don't be angry with them. Ask yourself the question, "Why is this person acting like this?" Maybe they are having a bad day, or maybe they just don't know how to act. That is not your problem, it is theirs! Quickly deal with them, and detach yourself as soon as possible. Ask yourself the question, "What do I need to do to take care of 'self'?" Then do what is necessary. Do not react to someone else's ignorance. Recognize that this is a set-up to steal your joy! Instead of acting harshly, switch the roles! Answer in your sweetest, kindest tone. Remember the saying, "It takes two to tango." If you refuse to argue, there is no argument. Don't sweat the small stuff! There is a bigger picture: your success!

Throughout the day, stay focused on your plans. Do not allow other people to distract you. Remember, you must take care of "self." Make a conscious effort to maintain your direction. I created an affirmation that helps me to stay grounded: *"My focus is my focus and my focus doesn't change. There's nothing you can do to make my focus rearrange."* I say this to myself throughout the day to keep me on track. You can say it too! You can also make up your own affirmations. Speak over your life; tell yourself, "I'm successful! I'm going to make it! I can do all things!" Become your own coach, and lead yourself mentally in the direction you want to go. Wherever your mind goes, your life is sure to follow!

Always be positive! Remember you have the power to label your situation. If you label it good, it will be good. If you label it bad, it will be bad. Change your perspective, and you will ultimately change your life!

Take time to learn about your "self." Determine what makes you happy, and begin to do those things. Enjoy life, and enjoy the journey! Rough times will not last, but while they're here, learn to enjoy them. Gain the philosophy of milking the cow.

Milk the good out of every circumstance that comes your way. We have to become like children to enjoy life. You can lock a child in his room and put him on punishment. Take away his radio, television, and his phone. Then let an hour go by and peek back into the child's room. You will find the kid turning his books into spaceships and making pencils action figures. The child learns to have fun even during his punishment. We must do the same and learn to enjoy life no matter what happens! Turn the storm into your playground, and then you will control the weather!

Continue working on "self." Go back to school, study and research how you can improve your talents. Don't just think about it, do it! Read positive books daily. Enhance and uplift your mind by learning new concepts and new experiences.

Join a religious group or church, and fellowship with other positive people. Read your Bible or other religious materials, and learn more about your "Higher Power." Be the best *you* that you know how to be! Go out your way to be kind, loving, and generous. Help people throughout your day achieve their goals. Do unto others as you would have them do unto you, and witness the energy you create around you! People will begin to be kind, loving, and generous to you.

Record your progress on your mission to "change." Congratulate yourself when you make progress, and reward yourself! Shower "self" with as much love, care, and compassion as you can give.

Don't forget to watch your health. Monitor what you eat and exercise daily. Fix your hair, get your nails done, and treat yourself to a facial. Then stand in front of the mirror, and admire the results! *Smile.*

Do your best to always dress well, and keep yourself well-groomed. Let your light radiate throughout the universe. You are special! You deserve it!

I really enjoyed our time together. I pray that these techniques and the information I've provided will help advance your life. Remember, you are in control. You now have the keys you need to drive the car. Place the keys in the ignition by applying these principles and techniques to your life. Don't just read this book once; read it again and again, until the words become one with you! Pass this book on. Share it with friends, and practice the techniques together. I promise you, things will begin to work out positively for you.

I look forward to meeting you again on the next road in our journey. Don't forget to pick up *Permission to Dream*. You are now ready for the next level! Congratulations!

Let's close this chapter with a short prayer: *"God, I thank You for helping me recognize how I can become a better 'self.' Help me to apply these techniques to my life, and enlighten me to new techniques and strategies that can help me improve myself. Empower me to become the best me I can possibly be! My desire is to make You proud. Strengthen me, lead me, and guide me, all the days of my life. Amen."*

CHAPTER QUESTIONS

1) What activities can you do in the morning to ensure your day will start off right?
2) What activities can you do on your way to work, or on your way to your destination, to give you energy to get through the day?
3) What can you do to combat negative feelings when they approach?
4) What can you do to turn your situation around, if you encounter an obstacle during the day?
5) What can you do to sustain your peace, if someone tries to irritate you?

WRITING ASSIGNMENT

Write a schedule of your day and the things you will do each day to work on "self." Include some of the techniques we discussed in this chapter.

AFTERWORD

I hope you have enjoyed this journey, and are now experiencing your new life, healed and restored. Don't stop here! Continue to work on "self." If you fall short, or you mess up, don't stay stuck! Dust yourself off and begin again. We all fall short at one point or another in our lives, yet the race is won by those who continue to run! Never stop running! You will arrive at your final destination shortly.

I am very proud of you! It took great courage to arrive where we are now. Very few who have encountered the troubles that we have are able to make it out of bondage. Congratulations, you have opened the prison doors of your mind and emotions. Soon you will follow, and physically walk out of the prison doors into society .

Life is going to be great! You will successfully begin again! This time your house will be built on a strong foundation. This time your success will last!

Remember, you are not alone on this journey. There are so many of us taking the same steps as you are. Please continue on to the next book in the *Voices of Consequences Enrichment Series*, entitled *Permission to Dream*. This book will show you the next set of techniques you can use to find your purpose and accomplish your dreams.

Congratulations on your success. May God forever keep you and bless you.

Love,
Jamila T. Davis.

REFERENCES

INTRODUCTION
Casarjian, Robin. House of Healing. Boston: Lionheart Press, 1995

CHAPTER ONE
Beattie, Melody. Codependent No More. Center City, Minnesota: Hazelden, 1987.
Narcotics Anonymous. California: World Service Office Inc., Van Nuys, 1988.
Williamson, Marianne. A Return to Love. New York: Harper Collins Publishers, 1992.

CHAPTER TWO
Beattie, Melody. Codependent No More. Center City, Minnesota: Hazelden, 1987.
The New King James Version Bible. Nashville, Tennessee: Thomas Nelson Inc., 1982.
Meyer, Joyce. Managing Your Emotions. New York: Hachette Book Company USA, 1997.
Williamson, Marianne. A Return To Love. New York: Harper Collins Publishers, 1992.

CHAPTER THREE
Beattie, Melody. Codependent No More. Center City, Minnesota: Hazelden, 1987.
The New King James Version Bible. Nashville, Tennessee: Thomas Nelson Inc., 1982.

Meyer, Joyce. Battlefield of The Mind. New York: Hachette
    Book Company, 1995.

CHAPTER FOUR

Beattie, Melody. Codependent No More. Center City,
    Minnesota: Hazelden, 1987.
The New King James Version Bible. Nashville, Tennessee:
    Thomas Nelson Inc., 1982.
Meyer, Joyce. Managing Your Emotions. New York: Hachette
    Book Company USA, 1997.
Narcotics Anonymous. California: World Service Office Inc.,
    Van Nuys, 1988.

CHAPTER FIVE

The New King James Version Bible, Nashville, Tennessee:
    Thomas Nelson Inc., 1982

CHAPTER SIX

Beattie, Melody. Codependent No More. Center City,
    Minnesota: Hazelden, 1987.
The New King James Version Bible. Nashville, Tennessee:
    Thomas Nelson Inc., 1982.
Casarjian, Robin. House of Healing. Boston: Lionheart Press,
    1995.
Meyer, Joyce. Battlefield of the Mind. New York: Hachette Book
    Company USA, 1995.
Meyer, Joyce. Managing Your Emotions. New York: Hachette
    Book Company USA, 1997.

CHAPTER SEVEN

The New King James Version Bible, Nashville, Tennessee: Thomas Nelson Inc., 1982.

Casarjian, Robin. House of Healing. Boston: Lionheart Press, 1995.

Meyer, Joyce.. Battlefield of The Mind. New York: Hachette Book Company USA, 1997.

CHAPTER EIGHT

Allen, James. As A Man Thinketh. Raddord, VA: Wilder Publications, 2007.

Byrne, Rhonda. The Secret. New York: Atria Books, 2006.

The New King James Version Bible, Nashville, Tennessee: Thomas Nelson Inc., 1982.

Meyer, Joyce. Battlefield of The Mind. New York: Hachette Book Company USA, 1997.

CHAPTER NINE

Beattie, Melody. Codependent No More. Center City, Minnesota: Hazelden, 1987.

The New King James Version Bible, Nashville, Tennessee: Thomas Nelson Inc., 1982.

Meyer, Joyce. Battlefield of The Mind. New York: Hachette Book Company USA, 1995..

Meyer, Joyce. Managing Your Emotions, New York: Hachette Book Company USA, 1997

Peale, Norman Vincent. The Power of Positive Thinking. Prentice Hall, 1996.

CHAPTER TEN

Beattie, Melody. Codependent No More. Center City, Minnesota: Hazelden, 1987.

Byrne, Rhonda. The Secret. New York: Atria Books, 2006.

CHAPTER ELEVEN

Canfield, Jack, Hansen, Mark, and Hewitt, Les. The Power of Focus. Deerfield Beach Florida: Peale, Health Communications Inc., 2000.

CHAPTER TWELVE

Beattie, Melody. Beyond Codependency. Center City, Minnesota: Hazelden. 1989.

The New King James Version Bible, Nashville, Tennessee: Thomas Nelson Inc., 1982.

Canfield, Jack, Hansen, Mark, and Hewitt, Les. The Power of Focus. Deerfield Beach Florida: Peale, Health Communications Inc., 2000.

Peale, Norman Vincent. The Power of Positive Thinking. Prentice Hall, 1996.

Voices International Publications Presents

$\mathcal{V}oices_{of}$
CONSEQUENCES
ENRICHMENT SERIES
CREATED BY: JAMILA T. DAVIS

Permission to Dream:
12 Points to Discovering Your Life's Purpose and Recapturing Your Dreams

ISBN: 978-09855807-4-2 Textbook
ISBN: 978-09855807-5-9 Workbook/Journal
ISBN: 978-09855807-6-6 Curriculum Guide

Permission to Dream is a nondenominational, faith-based, instruction manual created to inspire incarcerated women to discover their purpose in life and recapture their dreams. In a way readers can identify with and understand, this book provides strategies they can use to overcome the stigma and barriers of being an ex-felon.

This book reveals universal laws and proven self-help techniques that successful people apply in their everyday lives. It helps readers identify and destroy bad habits and criminal thinking patterns, enabling them to erase the defilement of their past.

Step-by-step this book empowers readers to recognize their talents and special skill sets, propelling them to tap into the power of "self" and discover their true potential, and recapture their dreams.

After reading *Permission To Dream*, readers will be equipped with courage and tenacity to take hold of their dreams and become their very best!

INTERNATIONAL PUBLICATIONS
"Changing Lives One Page At A Time."
www.vocseries.com

Voices International Publications Presents

$\mathcal{V}oices_{of}$
CONSEQUENCES
ENRICHMENT SERIES
CREATED BY: JAMILA T. DAVIS

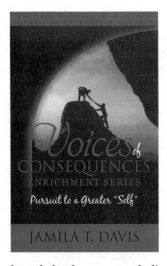

Pursuit to A Greater "Self:" 12 Points to Developing Good Character and HealthyRelationships

ISBN: 978-09855807-7-3 Textbook
ISBN: 978-09855807-8-0 Workbook/Journal
ISBN: 978-09855807-9-7 Curriculum Guide

Pursuit to A Greater "Self" is a non-denominational, faith-based, instruction manual created to help incarcerated women develop good character traits and cultivate healthy relationships.

This book is filled with real-life examples that illustrate how good character traits have helped many people live a more prosperous life, and how deficient character has caused others to fail. These striking examples, along with self-help strategies revealed in this book, are sure to inspire women to dethrone bad character traits and develop inner love, joy, peace, patience, kindness, generosity, faithfulness, gentleness and self-control. This book also instructs women how to utilize these positive character traits to cultivate healthy relationships.

After reading *Pursuit to A Greater "Self,"* readers will be inspired to let their light shine for the world to see that true reformation is attainable, even after imprisonment!

INTERNATIONAL PUBLICATIONS
"Changing Lives One Page At A Time."
www.vocseries.com

"Every negative choice we make in life comes with a consequence. Sometimes the costs we are forced to pay are severe!"
— Jamila T. Davis

She's All Caught Up is a real-life cautionary tale that exemplifies the powerful negative influences that affect today's youth and the consequences that arise from poor choices.

Young Jamila grew up in a loving middle class home, raised by two hardworking parents, the Davises, in the suburbs of Jamaica Queens, New York. Determined to afford their children the luxuries that they themselves never had, the Davises provided their children with a good life, hoping to guarantee their children's success.

At first it seemed as though their formula worked. Young Jamila maintained straight As and became her parents ideal "star child," as she graced the stage of Lincoln Center's Avery Fischer Hall in dance recitals and toured the country in a leading role in an off-Broadway play. All was copacetic in the Davis household until high school years when Jamila met her first love Craig- a 16 year old drug dealer from the Southside housing projects of Jamaica Queens.

As this high school teen rebels, breaking loose from her parents' tight reins, the Davises wage an "all-out" battle to save their only daughter whom they love so desperately. But Jamila is in too deep! Poisoned by the thorn of materialism, she lusts after independence, power and notoriety, and she chooses life in the fast lane to claim them.

When this good girl goes bad, it seems there is no turning back! Follow author, Jamila T. Davis (creator of the Voices of Consequences Enrichment Series) in her trailblazing memoir, *She's All Caught Up!*

DECEMBER 2012
ISBN: 978-09855807-3-5
www.voicesbooks.com

VOICES
INTERNATIONAL PUBLICATIONS

ORDER FORM

Mail to: 196-03 Linden Blvd.
St. Albans, NY 11412
or visit us on the web @
www.vocseries.com

QTY	Title	Price
	Unlocking the Prison Doors	14.95
	Unlocking the Prison Doors Workbook/Journal	14.95
	Permission to Dream	14.95
	Permission to Dream Workbook/Journal	14.95
	Pursuit to A Greater "Self"	14.95
	Pursuit to A Greater "Self" Workbook/Journal	14.95
	Total For Books	
	20% Inmate Discount -	
	Shipping/Handling +	
	Total Cost	

* Shipping/Handling 1-3 books 4.95
4-9 books 8.95
* Incarcerated individuals receive a 20% discount on each book purchase.
* Forms of Accepted Payments: Certified Checks, Institutional Checks and Money Orders.
* Bulk rates are available upon requests for orders of 10 books or more.
* Curriculum Guides are available for group sessions.
* All mail-in orders take 5-7 business days to be delivered. For prison orders, please
allow up to (3) three weeks for delivery.

SHIP TO:

Name: _____

Address: _____

_____

_____

City: _____

State: _____ Zip: _____